Comments on other *Amazing Stories* from readers & reviewers

"Tightly written volumes filled with lots of wit and humour about famous and infamous Canadians."
Eric Shackleton, *The Globe and Mail*

"The heightened sense of drama and intrigue, combined with a good dose of human interest is what sets Amazing Stories *apart."*
Pamela Klaffke, *Calgary Herald*

"This is popular history as it should be... For this price, buy two and give one to a friend."
Terry Cook, a reader from Ottawa, on ***Rebel Women***

"Glasner creates the moment of the explosion itself in graphic detail...she builds detail upon gruesome detail to create a convincingly authentic picture."
Peggy McKinnon, *The Sunday Herald*, on ***The Halifax Explosion***

"It was wonderful...I found I could not put it down. I was sorry when it was completed."
Dorothy F. from Manitoba on ***Marie-Anne Lagimodière***

"Stories are rich in description, and bristle with a clever, stylish realness."
Mark Weber, *Central Alberta Advisor*, on ***Ghost Town Stories II***

"A compelling read. Bertin...has selected only the most intriguing tales, which she narrates with a wealth of detail."
Joyce Glasner, *New Brunswick Reader*, on ***Strange Events***

"The resulting book is one readers will want to share with all the women in their lives."
Lynn Martel, *Rocky Mountain Outlook*, on ***Women Explorers***

AMAZING STORIES

PIERRE ELLIOTT TRUDEAU

AMAZING STORIES

PIERRE ELLIOTT TRUDEAU

The Fascinating Life of Canada's Most Flamboyant Prime Minister

BIOGRAPHY

by Stan Sauerwein

PUBLISHED BY ALTITUDE PUBLISHING CANADA LTD.
1500 Railway Avenue, Canmore, Alberta T1W 1P6
www.altitudepublishing.com
1-800-957-6888

First published 2004

Publisher	Stephen Hutchings
Associate Publisher	Kara Turner
Series Editor	Jill Foran
Editor	Dianne Smyth
Digital colouration	Scott Manktelow

We acknowledge the financial support of the Government of Canada through the Book Publishing Industry Development Program (BPIDP) for our publishing activities.

Altitude GreenTree Program 
Altitude Publishing will plant twice as many trees as were used in the manufacturing of this product.

National Library of Canada Cataloguing in Publication Data

Sauerwein, Stan, 1952-
Pierre Elliott Trudeau / Stan Sauerwein.

(Amazing stories)
Includes bibliographical references.
ISBN 1-55153-945-4

1. Trudeau, Pierre Elliott, 1919-2000. 2. Canada--Politics and government--1963-1984. 3. Prime ministers--Canada--Biography. I. Title. II. Series: Amazing stories (Canmore, Alta.)

FC626.T7S29 2004 971.064'4'092 C2004-902101-X

Printed and bound in Canada by Friesens
2 4 6 8 9 7 5 3

Cover: Pierre Elliott Trudeau wins the 1968 Liberal leadership in 1968 and becomes the Prime Minister of Canada.

To Pierre Elliott Trudeau's children,
Justin, Michel, Sacha, and Sarah

Contents

Prologue

Arab volunteer soldiers ignored the curiosity of his dirty canvas backpack and without asking questions, helped the young stranger climb into their truck. His kuffiyeh *headdress might have been why. He had a bushy brown beard and it gave him a pharaonic profile. Perhaps it was because he was deeply tanned. Whatever the reason, the young man nonchalantly settled into the excited knot of would-be warriors without a problem, ready to enjoy his 60-kilometre ride.*

It was May 1948, and Palestine was convulsed in war over the new state of Israel. Amman was the second Middle Eastern stop on the hitchhiker's trek towards the Far East. It was a tempest of foreign press and frightened Arabs. He was glad to leave it behind and decidedly pleased with his ingenuity regarding transportation.

Travel as a foreigner without proper documents was risky, but the 29-year-old student didn't care. A chance to see the Holy City outweighed any possibility of danger. As the troop truck crossed the Jordan River over the Allenby Bridge and followed the highway through Jericho, he checked the directions he'd been given to a Dominican monastery.

None of the Palestinian Army blockades, which he had

been told to expect, had threatened his ride. Upon reaching the walls of Jerusalem, he grabbed his pack and lunged from the moving truck towards the outskirts of the Old City. All the Biblical stories the Jesuits had taught him during years of classes at Collège Jean-de-Brébeuf in Montréal now flooded his mind in a tumble of memories. He was excited at the thought of touching the dusty stones, at walking the same narrow passageways Christ may have trod. He wandered through the Old City, lost in his imaginings, and by the time he finally found the monastery, he was blithely unaware of what was happening around him. But the crack of gunshots sobered him up.

Caught in Israeli–Arab crossfire near the monastery doors, he dove to the ground as did the frightened Arabs and Jews clogging the sidewalks around him. Feeling naked and vulnerable, he had no choice but to belly-crawl towards sanctuary. Once there, he pounded frantically on the monastery door.

When the street returned to normal after several hours, the young man decided he was ready to explore again. His Dominican host urged caution, and for good reason. Just a few moments after the priest gave him his blessing, the hitchhiker found himself in the middle of conflict one more time. It was as if the shooting had been choreographed. Instead of a crawl back to the monastery, though, he charged through the gauntlet of bullets carrying his pack like a football. To rifle-toting Arab soldiers, the bearded man looked exactly like a panicked enemy fighter with explosives. So, they pounced.

Prologue

It seemed Allah had given them a gift! With two passports, they knew their captive had *to be a Jewish spy, even if his odd name — Pierre Elliott Trudeau — said otherwise.*

Chapter 1
A Young Boy Discovers His Inner Strength

His flaws were many. But they were glorious. During his lifetime, the nation both abhorred and adored him. He was a statesman for his season. In many ways he was a chimera, haunting their dreams. A chimera that would continue casting its shadow through the daily lives of every Canadian for uncounted generations to come.

Pierre Elliott Trudeau was also an enigma. Despite his federalist vision of Canada, strengthened through its diversity rather than antagonistically riven by it, he was first and foremost a proud French Canadian. The French factor and an early trauma of loss had shaped him. And, through him, it also helped create a more modern Canada.

He'd grown-up in a household where Québec's two language realities merged seamlessly. It was a hybrid world, where questions might be asked in one language and answered in another. A household where Catholic prayers were whispered in French, and where dinner table politics, usually Tory, were argued in English.

His father, Charles-Emile, came from humble stock south of Montréal near the village of Saint-Michel-de-Napierville. Unlike Pierre's illiterate grandfather Joseph, who farmed on the south shore of the St. Lawrence River the same way nine generations of Trudeaus had done before him, Charlie reflected more of his mother's side of the family. Joseph's wife, Malvina, was a woman of determination. Her own father had been mayor of his village and her brother had been a doctor. Joseph and Malvina had 13 children, but five died in infancy.

To ensure his offspring had the opportunity for a good education, Joseph sold his farm and moved his brood to Saint-Rémi when Charlie was still quite young. Joseph hoped that in Montréal his children could be educated at a Jesuit classical college. The move had the desired effect. Of their eight surviving children, two became lawyers and one a dentist.

When still a teenager studying in Montréal, Charlie met Grace Elliott, the woman who would become Pierre's mother. She, too, was born into an enterprising family. Her father,

Philip Armstrong Elliott, had been a saloonkeeper and real estate speculator in downtown Montréal. Her family was of Scottish origin, but the Elliotts had a French history dating back to the British Empire Loyalists who settled in Québec. She'd attended the Dunham Ladies College in the Eastern Townships where, though a Catholic, she was "finished" alongside the daughters of Québec's Anglo-Protestant establishment.

The two were complete opposites. Charlie was boisterous and loud. He lived every day with gusto. Grace, on the other hand, was perfectly named. She was contemplative, refined, and frugal. In 1915, after a 10-year courtship, they finally could afford to marry. Charlie became a lawyer and ran a small practice alongside his brother and brother-in-law. However, simply being a lawyer in Montréal at that time didn't make you wealthy. Particularly if you were French. The Anglo-Protestant establishment had a tight grip on big business in Québec. The best clients usually turned to English-speaking lawyers, which left Charlie scraping the bottom of the barrel for the less lucrative work. He resented the discrimination he suffered.

When Britain went to war, Charlie joined the ranks of the French-Canadian objectors who refused to fight in what they saw as just another of England's imperialist adventures abroad. Charlie was hungry for a chance to prove himself the equal of any English businessman. He felt being a "second-class" lawyer would make him neither rich nor happy, so he cast about for a different career path and landed on a novel plan. He'd rely on the incredible popularity of a new invention, the automobile.

An American named Henry Ford had managed to break the U.S. patent held by George Baldwin Selden on internal combustion engines. After Ford's legal battle, anyone with the money and the will could manufacture autos without Selden's patented royalty. Ford had been cranking out Model T automobiles from his assembly plant in Walkerville, Ontario, for buyers across the British Empire since 1904. The $850 autos were everywhere. Charlie knew they would all need gasoline, towing, and repairs. His idea was to form a club that offered a $10 membership with discounts on these necessary services. He decided to call it the Automobile Owners' Association.

To get his idea off the ground, Charlie borrowed money from his friends and from his reluctant father-in-law, Philip. During the business start-up period, Grace pinched pennies to run the household while Charlie battled formidable class barriers to break into the English-speaking business world. For several years their future was dicey. But they were young and optimistic, like so many other enterprising French Canadians at that time. The French bourgeoisie — lawyers, accountants, doctors, and shopkeepers — were scrambling to build a new vision for themselves.

Within a year of their wedding, Grace gave birth to her first son but he died in infancy. Such tragedy wasn't uncommon at the time, so it didn't stop the Trudeaus from having more children in rapid succession. Suzette was born in 1918. Joseph Philippe Pierre Yves Elliott came along a year later, on October 18, 1919. Two years after that Charles Elliott (Tip) arrived.

Montréal was wild and wide open in the 1920s, a city of vibrant though often illegal nightlife. Stories of mobsters, street gangs, and corrupt politicians appeared on the newspapers' front pages as often as stories about the latest NHL victories of the Montréal Canadiens.

Charlie's character seemed a perfect match for the times. He opened a garage for the slowly growing membership of his association and took to the knuckle-crunching duties of a grease monkey without qualms, often jumping in to help his staff pump gas or fix cars. He was a curser and a shouter, willing to resort to fisticuffs with his mechanics if he didn't get his way. After long shifts in the garage he would often wander over to the Club Saint Denis to drink and play cards. This social fraternity was formed by French Canadians who were discouraged from joining the English men's clubs in Montréal. If he drank too much, Charlie showed a darker side, but for the most part he was gregarious and fun loving and attracted an equally boisterous group of friends.

Charlie soon had some success with his business, at least enough to afford a modest yellow brick home near the Montréal city limits. The house was part of a row of similar dwellings that had been built six years before Pierre was born, and Charlie made it a friendly place, often inviting his friends there to share dinner. The impromptu gatherings transformed the petite house at 5779 rue Durocher into something of a party place. The street was home to an eclectic mix of religions and nationalities: Jews, Protestants, Catholics, Irish, Scots, and French Canadians. Francophones and Anglophones both clustered just inside the border of the middle-class suburb of Outremont. When the house overflowed with revellers, the laughter would echo through the streets and usually attract the eager participation of neighbours as well.

Only a few blocks away from the Trudeau home, the Académie Querbes reflected the cultural mosaic on rue Durocher, at least partly. It offered Catholic families a choice of English or French instruction for the first three elementary school grades. English was the second choice for most parents, however, so those classes had fewer students. That meant the pupils shared the same room and teacher for all three grades, much like a country schoolhouse. The English classroom is where young Pierre Trudeau found himself on his first day of school.

Académie Querbes was perhaps the first place Pierre publicly showed his independent side, a trait that later exhibited itself in fearlessness when he was confronted with rules he found unfair. On his first day there, he discovered his best friend, Gerald O'Connor, had been given a privilege for no reason other than his heritage. Gerald, no brighter than

Pierre, was seated in the second grade row simply because he came from an English-speaking family. That irked young Pierre. First-year training focussed on English, so the seating may have made sense to the teacher. But it didn't to Pierre. He was just as fluent as Gerald in English, Québec's other language, but Pierre's household was known to be French Canadian by the Académie Querbes' staff.

Pierre liked Gerald. He wanted to be near his friend in that crowded class of strangers. After his first day, Pierre complained to his father at dinner about the injustice. Charlie just shook his head. Perhaps it would serve as an early lesson for his son, demonstrating the imbalance of Québec's cultural environment.

"It's not fair," Pierre told his father. "I should be in the second grade too."

"Then it's simple. Go see the principal and ask him to put you in the second grade."

"Couldn't *you* ask him, papa?"

"No. It's your problem. Knock on his door and ask him yourself."

Often, when his children faced a challenge he thought they ought to be able to handle themselves, Charlie would refuse to act, perhaps thinking it was better they learn how to do it themselves. The next day, timid little Pierre talked himself through his anxiety and bravely entered the principal's office. He was barely tall enough to be seen on the other side of the headmaster's wide desk.

"I want to move to the second grade row," he announced in French, his voice cracking.

"Do you? Second grade is for children who already speak English. Your papa is French."

"What difference does that make?" Pierre clenched his fists at his sides and summoned his courage. "It's not fair! I can talk English just as good," he said, switching to his second language.

"Well," the principal said, correcting Pierre's grammar.

"Well," Pierre nodded.

"Then move to the other row."

Pierre was amazed. His promotion to the second grade was immediate. He'd been dreading a test of his ability, but the principal asked no more questions. It was done. Just like that. He only had to stand up for himself. It was a lesson he never forgot.

Besides building self-reliance, Charlie insisted that Pierre and his brother Tip overcome their physical weaknesses as well. Pierre was shy and puny. In his younger years he often broke down in a public show of tears. This irked Charlie, who insisted his son show some discipline. In an attempt to please his father, Pierre joined in the roughest games — hockey and lacrosse. He took to doing regular sets of callisthenics outdoors on their tiny lawn, even in the coldest Montréal winters. He also took boxing lessons from his father. While he may not have been the strongest boy on the block, he was definitely the most committed. Pierre gained co-ordination, became nimble and wiry, and developed a lightning-fast right cross. Though his shyness hadn't diminished, and he was still reluctant to stand out from the crowd, the discipline his father insisted upon gave Pierre a sense of courage. He never backed down from a dare on rue Durocher. He had to be pushed into the limelight, but once he accepted a challenge there was no stopping him. Despite his size, he was the boy left standing after any test of mettle, and so became his larger friends' improbable defender against street toughs.

Though money continued to be tight at rue Durocher, Charlie and Grace managed to buy a Spartan summerhouse in Lac Tremblant while Pierre was still young enough to invade the woods and pretend. With his fertile child's imagination, Pierre was a *coureur de bois* in deerskin, an explorer without a map. He took to the rough cottage life in the woods with the same enthusiasm he'd shown at home in Montréal. The long summer days at the lake kindled a life-long love for canoeing and the wilderness. He discovered an inner strength, a faith in himself, and an independence that he would later call upon during some of the darkest days of his life.

By the time Canada entered the Great Depression, Charlie had accumulated a string of service stations. In the early 1930s, when other men were forced to leave their families behind and trundle across the country in search of a job, Pierre's father managed to sell his stations to Imperial Oil for more than a million dollars, a sum equivalent to $11.4 million today. The Trudeaus were catapulted into the sheltered ranks of the wealthy at a time when the rest of Canada was plunged into a period of economic depression. Starvation was a desperate reality in the Prairie's dustbowl provinces, and destitution was commonplace on Montréal's streets. It was a time when tailors in Montréal worked 54-hour weeks for $40. And Charlie's mechanics had earned far less.

Charlie shifted his entrepreneurship to investment speculation and sports. He bought shares in the Sullivan Mines, became a part owner of the Belmont Park amusement complex, and got a share of the Montréal Royals baseball club. While his bank balance may have changed, Charlie's basic nature had not. He still loved his card playing and carousing with friends. He spent his money freely, promoting the careers of boxers he thought were promising and travelling widely to see their bouts. He also pulled up stakes at rue Durocher, now much too modest for his new stature, and changed the location of his regular rounds of parties to a new home on McCulloch Avenue, an upper-class street at the foot of Mount Royal.

All of Pierre's friends lived on rue Durocher, however, and Pierre was embarrassed by the vast difference between his family's new lifestyle and theirs. He was happy when, at 12 years old, he was enrolled at Collège Jean-de-Brébeuf. At this upscale school he was able to play side by side with the other boys as an equal. The burden of his recent shift in socioeconomic class was not so obvious as it was when he played with the rue Durocher gang.

The private Jesuit-run school where Pierre would spend his teens immersed in a classical education opened its doors for the first time in 1928. Collège Jean-de-Brébeuf's namesake had been officially canonized the year before Pierre's 1931 enrollment. Many of Québec's upper class sent their children to Loyola, another school run by the Soldiers of Christ, where classes were taught in English, the language of business. But Brébeuf was perfect for Pierre. The stone edifice on Côte-Ste-Catherine, not far from his old Montréal neighborhood, reflected the missionary martyr's zeal in its teaching methods. French was the *only* language spoken there. The atmosphere was one of intellectual excellence. Students were encouraged in their religious devotion, but were also pressed to undertake a personal quest for enlightened self-development. The Brébeuf students were taught to think and to question, to love books, and to aspire to the best in themselves. Pierre gained valuable life lessons at Brébeuf.

An unspoken tradition at the school was a game of superiority. Senior classmen bullied the new recruits indiscriminately, and the younger freshmen were expected to like it or lump it. Not Pierre. Early in his Brébeuf days he displayed his disdain for the status quo. During one lunch period, a senior classmate plopped a banana into Pierre's soup. The slight newcomer immediately returned the gift. Challenged by the older and louder boy to settle this dispute in the schoolyard after lunch, Pierre agreed. He was used to dealing with street toughs on rue Durocher. This boy, in his pressed shirt, was just one more bully. The two boys scowled at each other all through the meal. Classmates whispered their encouragement as Pierre kept his cold stare frozen on his opponent. When the time came to take the argument outdoors, diminutive Pierre moved towards his larger opponent as though the battle was already won — in his favour. He wasn't being cocky. He'd just bloodied enough noses to be confident, and it showed.

The senior student stared down at the wiry freshman who had his fists clenched and ready at his sides. The larger boy must have wondered what was going on. This puny freshmen wasn't just ready, he was eager! By all rights he should have been terrified but instead he wore a thin smile. The senior student quickly decided his best course was retreat. He let Pierre off with a warning. Years later, in his memoirs, Pierre admitted to learning something important. That day he'd been very frightened, but learned "you can win some confrontations just by acting confident."

Outward bluster was one thing. Pierre discovered that facing his internal demons wasn't quite so simple. As time passed at Brébeuf, he felt guilty about the academic edge his privileged life was giving him. His friends had to study at crowded kitchen tables in tiny rue Durocher houses while he had a quiet bedroom of his own in Mount Royal. Was it fair for him to have privileges just because his father got lucky in business? Was it fair that his parents didn't worry about money anymore? Was it fair that he could buy any books he needed and read them at his leisure, while his old friends had to borrow books and hurry to read them?

These issues were difficult for Pierre to resolve, particularly because he so thoroughly enjoyed learning. He read voraciously and viewed the study requirements of his classes as a personal challenge. Did he skip a chapter in a textbook simply because it wouldn't be on a test? Absolutely not. It was in the textbook for a reason and he wanted to know why.

At Brébeuf, Pierre was in his element. He was bright. That intellectual strength helped him comfortably overcome his shyness. He was vocal in class, almost to the point of being a distraction as he questioned his teachers without fear and peppered their lessons with asides of his own. The wisecracks he made became artful forms of provocation, goading his teachers into debates. Oftentimes, the arguments in class slipped off topic into religion and ethnicity. Pierre, as a child of two languages, vacillated between anglophilia and anglophobia, exemplifying his unique upbringing. To the teachers at Brébeuf he was a trial. They began calling him *un catholique protestant* because his views never seemed to fit for long in either French or English camp. He constantly challenged their dicta and defended his right to freedom of thought — but even so, he never outright rejected the church's dogma.

By 1932, the issue of wealth and privilege that had

nagged him was creating a huge internal conflict for Pierre. The misery of the Depression was evident everywhere in Montréal. Nearly 30 percent of the population, an estimated 250,000 residents, were on relief. He saw the misery as he went to school and had trouble reconciling the inequity. That summer, he was relieved to learn that his father was taking the whole family, including his grandfather Elliott, on a European holiday. It gave him a break from his incredible burden of guilt.

Chapter 2
Shaped By Grief

Pierre spent the summer of 1932 on a holiday that would infect him permanently with wanderlust. Twelve-year-old Pierre, his parents, grandfather, 15-year-old sister Suzette, and 11-year-old brother Tip, travelled through Europe in style.

Pierre found himself adept at blending into any culture he encountered, getting by with only a handful of foreign phrases avidly memorized from the guidebooks. To Pierre, it was a game of creativity and intellect. He willingly faced desk clerks to order hotel rooms despite his age and his scant knowledge of their languages. He blissfully toured the museums and monuments, but in his adolescent naiveté was completely oblivious to the political foment in Europe at the time.

Hitler was known to Pierre only by the gleaming motorcycles the German soldiers rode on the highways.

By the time he returned to Montréal, he was imbued with an even greater desire to learn. His exposure to ancient history that summer seized him. Art, music, philosophy, literature — all had an equal place on his desk and in his life. Curiously, politics held no interest for him. He rarely read a newspaper or listened to the news on a radio, thinking current events a waste of study time. He maintained his love of sports, however, taking up skiing in winter and enjoying regular excursions to Lac Tremblant. For Pierre, time was an easy flow of fun during the next two years of his life. When he was 15, it all came to an abrupt end.

In April 1935, Charlie was visiting his beloved Montréal Royals at their summer training camp in Florida. After developing pneumonia, he died there.

With the news of his father's death, Pierre's carefree world instantly evaporated. All his childish dreams vanished — dreams of being a sea captain, an explorer, or an astronaut (he'd read about that curious space age occupation in a Jules Verne novel decades before it was popular). All it took was the trill of the telephone. His father's death suddenly put him at the head of the family. And, in that moment of despair, Pierre's outlook changed forever.

Life on McCulloch Avenue changed as well. In the three years before his death, Pierre's father had tripled the million dollars he had made from selling his gas stations. He left the family a $3 million dollar fortune, equivalent to more than $42 million today. But he could not leave them his gregarious nature. The Trudeau home grew quiet. Grace fell back upon the support of her Catholic faith and Pierre accompanied her daily to morning mass. "When my father was around, there was a great deal of effusiveness and laughter and kissing and hugging," he later described. After his father died, the atmosphere changed at home. There were no more parties, no swarms of athletes who visited at all hours to share victory stories and crude jokes. French disappeared from the Trudeau home, replaced almost exclusively by English.

Pierre withdrew deep within himself. He became quiet and, though he conducted himself with English politeness, non-communicative. On the streets he was different. He was a mouthy angry young man who deliberately provoked strangers into fistfights. It was as if he was trying to mirror the machismo of his father. Yet, he seemed to be experimenting with ways to show the world he was his own man. He rejected the countrified French his father had spoken and would not use the *patois* of the Québécois. Instead, he took diction lessons to learn the perfect accent of classical French. He played with his name. For a time he was Pierre-Philippe Trudeau. That changed to Pierre Esprit Trudeau, and that changed again to Pierre Elliott-Trudeau. Pierre was struggling to find an identity of his own. He was openly critical of the excessive drinking he had so often witnessed with his father. He gave up the populist sports Charlie had loved and instead focussed on solitary ones, diving and skiing, with the dedication of a perfectionist.

After his father's death, Pierre found himself more willing to accept the laudatory reminders of his Jesuit teachers that the students of Brébeuf were the *crème de la crème* of Québec society. He worried less, if at all, about how his old friends might view his wealth or the privileges it brought. In fact, as he had done with language and sports, he gravitated to the opposite extreme. He ran with a cheeky crowd of well-to-do children who called themselves *les snobs.*

His playful wisecracks and debating discourse with his teachers became disobedient disruptions in the classroom. Pierre now vaulted into arguments. He aggressively sought pleasure toying with abstract ideas. He used his intellect as a weapon, one that was sharpened by the debating tricks of sophistry and rhetoric the Jesuits had themselves taught him. In every verbal joust, it became more and more evident that having the last word was of ultimate importance to Pierre.

When Britain and France declared war on Germany on September 3, 1939, he still had a year to complete before graduating from Brébeuf. The Declaration of War began an intense period of racial conflict in Québec. Francophones in Québec looked upon the tension in Europe much the way others before them had during the First World War. They considered it a British conflict. It was none of *their* business. Pierre remembered his father talking of how he and many Quebecers had refused to go to war in earlier years. Pierre was determined not to enlist either. In a ploy used by many middle class Canadians, he enrolled in the Canadian Officers' Training Corps (COTC) and continued with his studies. The COTC program, aimed at training university undergraduates for officer commissions, required him to appear at the armory in Montréal twice a week for marching drill and to learn how to handle weapons.

He met his obligations, but not without showing his disdain and his feelings of superiority. During summer training at Camp Farnham, for example, he was detailed with a group of other COTC cadets to move shells. That day, Pierre and a detail of other young French-Canadian men stood at attention while their English cadet sergeant barked his instructions. When he finished, seven others in Pierre's group followed the orders but Pierre remained steadfastly in place.

"I said hump those shells now, cadet!" The sergeant ordered. "Get going!" Pierre didn't move.

"What's the matter with you? Are you deaf?" an observing cadet captain asked.

"*Je n'ai pas comprends.*"

A captain who had been observing the verbal joust shook his head and then repeated the order in faltering French.

"*Bon. Maintenant je vous comprends,*" Pierre answered. "Remember that here in Canada, we are entitled to be commanded in two languages."

Graduating from Brébeuf in 1940, he followed in his

father's footsteps and enrolled at the Université de Montréal to study law. Pierre adapted quickly to the freethinking atmosphere, well prepared by his Jesuit training to pursue higher education independently. He continued to voice his objection to military service as the war went on.

Mackenzie King, seeking election as a Liberal, had vowed never to impose compulsory military service in Canada or to repeat the conscription crisis that had rocked Québec with riots in 1917. Yet, once in power, he turned to English-speaking Canada for support in a referendum that relieved him of his promise. French Canadians, Pierre included, were outraged. Nearly 73 percent of them had voted against conscription. Pierre took to the streets in marches and meetings opposing the measure. With his debating skills now honed by post-secondary study, he also spoke out against conscription during a 1942 by-election in Outremont. It was his only foray into politics during his youth. A lawyer named Jean Drapeau, who years later would become mayor of Montréal, was running against the Liberal candidate, Major-General Léo LaFlèche. Pierre took to the microphone and shouted to a crowd of angry Montréalers:

"There is currently a government which wants to invoke conscription and a people who will never accept it. If we are not a democracy, we should start a revolution without delay... they are asking our people to commit suicide. Citizens of Québec, don't stand around blubbering. Long live the [Drapeau] flag of liberty!"

The people didn't revolt over the issue, however, and LaFlèche won the election. Discouraged, perhaps by what he saw as weakness in the electorate, Pierre turned away from the issue and back to his studies. However, he soon found life at the university boring and unfulfilling. It seemed that he had adopted his father's early disinterest in law as a career. "The law school was abysmal," he later wrote. "The courses consisted entirely of parochial instruction in petty law with none of the large issues addressed." He decided law school training in Québec readied graduates for a "two-bit life among unthinking people."

Pierre fed his sense of adventure in other ways. Expeditions. One summer, when he was about 20, he organized what — even today — could be considered an odyssey. Pierre, with his friend Guy Viau and two others, decided to paddle to Hudson Bay. Travelling the old *voyageur* route, they headed westward in canoes along the Ottawa River. Their quest took them northward, across Lake Timiskaming and, eventually, to the Harricana River. As their Québecois forebears had done, they followed it all the way to James Bay.

On another trip, they toured the Gaspé Peninsula on foot. As it was wartime, that trip had some interesting twists. The young men travelled with very little money. They looked like vagabonds. The group slept in barns and empty classrooms because soldiers guarding the coast enforced a curfew on the riverbanks at night. Out of an arcane fear of invasion, the government had ordered the small Gaspé villages to abide by a general blackout after sunset. The journey undertaken by the young men was highly unusual and provocative. They left themselves open to repeated military harassment. Time and time again they had to prove to English-speaking privates from Saskatchewan that they were not, in fact, the leading edge of a German strike force. Pierre relished the insanity of it all and used every opportunity to mock the military absurdities he witnessed. His sense of humour had an obnoxious side. On one occasion, he and a friend dressed up in moth-eaten Franco-Prussian uniforms (last worn in 1870) that they'd found in an attic, complete with pointed steel helmets. Shouting phrases in German that Pierre had learned in Europe when he was 12, they roared across the countryside on a motorcycle, taunting hapless army outposts and deliberately frightening friends.

In the meantime, Pierre continued his studies and completed his law degree. He began to article for a downtown Montréal law firm. The working life he encountered was the "proof in the pudding" for his earlier opinions. Pierre was exasperated by the tedium. Rather than adapt to it, he focussed on mindless diversions, such as finding a new place to eat lunch every day. He was miserable. He felt his career choice was probably the biggest mistake of his life. But what else could he pursue?

It seemed he'd never find the satisfaction he wanted or the call of purpose. It was a happenstance that shifted him. One day he was listening to someone recite a poem. The person was reading one of Cyrano de Bergerac's tirades. Suddenly, in the words of the last line, Pierre found a way to express who he was. He knew then that he wanted to be like Cyrano:

> *… to sing, to laugh, to dream,*
> *To walk in my own way …*
> *Free to cock my hat where I choose …*
> *To fight or write. To travel any road*
> *Under the sun or the stars …*
> *And if my nature wants that which grows*
> *Towering to heaven like the mountain pine,*
> *I'll climb, not high perhaps, but all alone!*

During his time as a law student, though in his twenties and at an age when young men usually leave home to find some independence, Pierre continued to live at home. It wasn't as if he needed to keep his lonely mother company. Grace had a country girl living in the house as her maid. And her handyman driver, Grenier, was considered almost family (he worked for the Trudeaus through four decades). Pierre lived there more because Grace had become the love of his life. He treasured his time with his mother.

Though he dated the opposite sex, romances with the genteel French-Canadian girls approved by his mother were few and far between. They seemed pale and bland to him. Pierre had no desire to build long-term bonds and rarely let intimacy creep into his relationships. He wasn't particularly attractive to women either. Self-conscious about being short and thin, he also had a terrible complexion. His face displayed the remnants of the acne he had suffered as a teenager. Pierre's concern about his appearance expressed itself socially as severe shyness, which he disguised with immature antics.

At parties he might provoke loud arguments on subjects he didn't really care about, peppering his conversation with sarcasm, or he might suddenly do handstands in a crowded room just to gain attention. As a young man, his one foray towards marriage ended abysmally when he publicly taunted his fiancée with a cruel put-down during a dinner party. "If I had hips like yours, I'd give up cake," he said. His voice may have been jocular but she knew he meant every word. His fiancée's hopes collapsed in embarrassment, and so ended any prospects for marriage. Afterwards, free of any commitment, Pierre left Montréal.

Chapter 3 Finding a Meaning in Life

In September 1944, a month before his 25th birthday, Pierre enrolled at Harvard University in Cambridge, Massachusetts. It was clearly a way of delaying his development, allowing him to put off the strangling need to settle in an occupation, find a suitable wife, and raise a family. Pierre didn't view it as escape, though. He believed he was moving forward, away from his earlier mistake of following so closely in his father's footsteps. "I always regarded regret as a useless emotion," he wrote. "I have never looked back at my mistakes, except to make sure I would not repeat them."

At Harvard, Pierre quickly realized life in Montréal had insulated him from the world. The other students were more sophisticated and had a deeper understanding of broader issues, things he'd never had to consider in Québec. He determined to be more like other students, more urbane and conscious of the world around him. He pencilled a sign for his dorm room that said it all: Pierre Trudeau — Citizen of the World.

Pierre had only a vague notion of what he wanted to do for a career. Teaching was nearest to his ultimate, though still unformed, ideal. Before leaving Montréal, he had sought the advice of André Laurendeau, a writer he respected. Laurendeau told him that what Quebéc desperately needed was successful people with economic wisdom, professionals who could advise French-Canadian society and government. To Pierre, the counsel made sense. He certainly had one of the required criteria: plenty of money. All he needed was the expertise, and Harvard was the best place on the continent to attain it. For his masters program he decided to study political economy and government. True to Harvard's reputation, the courses were not just run-of-the-mill.

Wassily Leontief taught two of Pierre's eight courses. Leontief was a Russian émigré who was to win a Nobel Prize for his input–output modelling of the American economy. Pierre also studied under Alvin Hansen, the most respected American apostle of Keynesianism (John Maynard Keynes was a titled English economist who advocated that recovery from a recession is best achieved by government programs to increase employment and spending). In addition, Pierre studied central banking in a course given by Joseph Schumpeter, a seminal analyst of business cycles.

The eight political science courses he took had equally impressive instructors. One of the highlights of Pierre's courses was his study with historian Charles McIlwain, who taught that there are some individual rights so sacrosanct that government should not be able to abuse them. Another course Pierre found particularly fascinating was taught by Carl Friedrich, an eminent constitutionalist. Without consciously trying, Pierre was filling his tool chest, not for a teaching career as much as for a political one. "I realized that the Québec of my time was away from the action, that it was living outside modern times," he wrote. "My studies at Harvard quickly confirmed my beliefs about individual freedom. The view that every human must remain free to shape his own destiny became for me a certainty and one of the pillars of the political thought I was working to develop."

At the age of 27, even holding his Harvard degree, Pierre still didn't know what he wanted to do. If it was teaching, though, it would have to be at the university level, and for that he knew a doctorate was necessary. He'd completed his exams and orals for a doctorate at Harvard, so all that remained was his dissertation.

To pursue a dissertation subject, he turned eastward. The Allied victory in Europe was declared May 8, 1945, so when he arrived in Paris to attend classes at Ecole Libre des Sciences Politiques, the city was still suffering the privations of war. Food and clothing continued to be rationed. Medical care was seriously hampered by insufficient quantities of drugs.

Ecole Libre des Sciences Politiques was an elitist institution that many offspring of the French bourgeoisie aspired to attend, including French-Canadian Pierre. But when he arrived he discovered he was most comfortable not with the French, but with the other Canadian students. Most of the students living with him at the Maison des étudiants du Canada were poor. Paris was in political foment and Pierre dived into the maelstrom enthusiastically.

With money to spend on food and entertainment, and with a solid base of Harvard training to call upon, he liberally salted his class time with parties and long evenings in street-side cafes and bistros. Gasoline was still being rationed, so aside from military vehicles, there were few automobiles on the streets of Paris. He was tremendously happy racing along its streets at breakneck speeds on his Harley-Davidson motorcycle and arguing arcane political theory many nights until dawn. Pierre, however, found the French patronizing to French Canadians and the courses offered in Paris inferior to his graduate work at Harvard. So, at the end of the university year, he decided to quit Paris and try the London School of Economics (LSE) instead.

Unlike the schools on the Continent, the LSE offered a remarkable mixture of nationalities and ideologies for Pierre to sample. At the time it was, as his aunt living in the village of Varengeville in the south of France said, "a famous school filled with black men and red women." The social experiment in Russia was fuelling a bonfire of political opinion at the LSE, and Pierre attached himself to one of Britain's most powerful spokesmen who was teaching there, Harold Laski. Laski, as it happened, was also the senior officer in the British Labour Party. "I wanted to know the roots of power. I wanted to know how governments work and why people obey." Everything Pierre had learned about law, economics, and political thought coalesced for him at the London School of Economics.

For his doctoral subject, Pierre eventually decided to write his dissertation on the interplay between Christianity and Marxism, two ideologies that were battling for the hearts of people in Asia. He settled on India as the locus for his thesis because he knew it had plenty of Canadian Catholic missionaries who would help him, and Marxists as well. He smugly determined to travel there at his leisure. Along the way he would just follow his nose, mixing with the people he encountered to learn about their lifestyles and habits. He'd backpack, travelling in third-class coaches on trains, on buses, and on cargo boats. The wanderlust he had first experienced as a 12-year-old on summer vacation with his father had re-emerged. Research for his dissertation was a handy excuse. He'd managed quite well on that trip with his father, and wondered if he could survive on his own in a remote Chinese province, not speaking a word of Chinese.

In spring 1948, he stuffed his backpack with casual clothes, journals, and unlimited expectations. He spent the first two months tramping through Eastern Europe as an early test of his ingenuity. Crossing some borders meant he had to make himself false documents, which he did surprisingly well most of the time. In one country, however, suspicious border guards were not fooled. Pierre was the guest in a dingy cell for a day before being deported. But by then he was open to experiences of all kinds.

His hair was long. He had a bushy beard that framed his aquiline nose and almond-shaped eyes, which gave him a curious kind of homogeneity that helped him fit in almost anywhere he went. By the time he'd reached Turkey at the end of that summer, Pierre had been to Poland, Czechoslovakia, Austria, Hungary, Yugoslavia, and Bulgaria. And he was ready for sights even more exotic.

In Turkey, he decided he wanted to visit the new state of Israel, whose independence had just been declared on May 14, 1948. Palestine, however, was a turmoil of religiously inspired fighting, and he needed a visa. Since Canada did not have an embassy in Ankara, Pierre took the second-best alternative. He visited the British Embassy and was given a British passport to attach to his Canadian one.

After visiting Beirut, he walked to Amman, the capital of what was then called Transjordan. The excitement was palpable in Amman and Pierre was after the latest news about the conflict. To get it, he sought out the international press, who had taken over the Philadelphia Hotel *en masse* as their base of operations. When he spoke with reporters he was amazed. They were a sober group, satisfied to cover the war from their hotel rooms without risking life and limb on the actual firing lines in Jerusalem. "We don't have the necessary travel documents," they told him. "And in any event, the road between Jericho and Jerusalem has just been blocked by Palestine forces. It's too risky."

Not having the necessary papers had stymied Pierre only once on his journey thus far, so he didn't see that as a major hurdle. As to the risk, he thought it was worth taking if it meant his prize would be a chance to visit the Holy City. He knew that, if he got there, he could call on the aid of a Dominican priest to steer him about safely, and he had received instructions on how to get to the monastery in Jerusalem from a priest in Beirut. Taking coffee in the main square in Amman, he contemplated his problem. The square was swarming with activity. For a while, sipping the sweet hot drink, he observed the ruckus of wailing Arab mothers who were surrounding a group of trucks loaded with Arab volunteer soldiers.

Appropriate with his plan to mingle wherever he travelled, Pierre had adopted the local style of clothing in Palestine. He'd been wearing a traditional Arab headdress as protection from the desert sun and realized he looked just like the volunteer soldiers. Without a moment's hesitation he ran forward, tossed his backpack up, and climbed into a truck. His transportation rolled on towards Jerusalem, unmolested by Palestine forces. Pierre unceremoniously leapt from the moving vehicle at the gates to the Old City and followed his written directions to the monastery. Again, he was undisturbed until he reached his destination, whereupon he was caught in a crossfire of bullets between Israeli and Arab fighters. Forced to belly crawl to safety inside the monastery, he visited with the Dominican priest until the gunfight was over. As he left to continue his exploration, he was captured by Palestinian soldiers and imprisoned. Pierre's two passports concerned the Arabs. They suspected he was a Jewish spy for the Haganah sent to monitor their troop strength. They kept him jailed for days with the threat of a death sentence.

Fortunately, the Dominican priest he'd come to visit had witnessed the arrest. After intense negotiations, the Arabs took the priest's word that Pierre was only a travelling student. They loaded him back into a truck bound for Jordan. On his arrival in Amman he remained in army custody with a new set of jailers, but they spoke English better than his previous captors. Seizing diplomacy as his only option, Pierre demanded to see the staff from the British Embassy. More serious negotiations ensued and, with a reprimand for his foolhardy behaviour, Pierre was finally released.

It wasn't the only time he'd have run-ins with the military on his "walk-about." He arrived in Pakistan soon after India had been split, and the border between Lahore and Amristsar was overrun with refugees. While in Afghanistan and Burma he walked through a countryside ripped by civil war. In Indochina, while travelling in a French convoy, Pierre saw the fierce fighting spirit of the Viet Cong first-hand when he was attacked by a patrol. In China he roamed freely about as troops of Mao Zedong and Chiang Kai-shek did battle in that country.

Through his year of wandering, Pierre had plenty of time to consider what his true destiny might be. He carefully thought about the values on which he would base the rest of his life. Pierre knew that he'd approached life in a very different way than most people. Others usually chose a profession and then sought specific training in that profession. Pierre, instead, went searching not for credentials, but for a basic understanding of the world. He was deeply committed to the ideals of freedom and free will, and to the Catholic faith as well. But instead of finding out who he was, Pierre was only discovering who he was not. He was not a lawyer. Not a philosopher. Perhaps, he admitted to himself, not a teacher either. If not, though, what?

Five years after leaving Montréal he returned, still undecided about himself and his life.

Chapter 4 Building the Foundation for Power

aurice Duplessis had been Québec's ultra conservative premier for three years before Trudeau left, and he regained power in 1944, just when Trudeau moved to Harvard. Le Chef, as he came to be known, was a demagogue in Québec. His Union Nationale government influence touched the lives of everyone. His policies of isolation for Québec had marginalized the province, in effect separating it from the rest of Canada and the world.

Trudeau was deeply disappointed to find Duplessis still securely in power. He had travelled the globe, witnessing many nations in an evolutionary process of rebuilding themselves. But that fervor had not yet touched his beloved province. Shortly after his return in April, he made an effort to reacquaint himself with old friends and met up with Gérard Pelletier. Pelletier was a reporter for the Montréal newspaper *Le Devoir*, and he was covering a workers' strike in the Eastern Townships. During the previous winter, grievances about pay scales and working conditions had precipitated a strike in the remote town of Asbestos. The government tried to settle the dispute with arbitration first and when that failed, with force. Workers who gathered to protest were silenced by police squads wielding clubs. The labour strife there had been dragging on for four months and Duplessis had announced anti-strike legislation to bring it to an end.

Trudeau drove Gérard to Asbestos in his battered sports car and travelled along with the reporter as he gathered information for stories. Like many people in Québec, Trudeau was sympathetic to the worker's situation and their fight for better conditions. During his three weeks in Asbestos, he found himself quickly changed from observer to participant. At a church hall meeting of miners, Trudeau took to the stand and delivered an impassioned speech so inflammatory it even alarmed Jean Marchand, the union leader organizing the strike. The workers were attracted to Trudeau immediately, and began calling him Saint Joseph in reference to the bushy beard he still wore, and to his zealous oratory.

From what he experienced in his travels and what he

learned in his post-graduate study, Trudeau had come to believe democracy was the highest form of government and federalism the highest form of democracy. He saw the events in Asbestos as democracy in action at its base root, and later described the strike as "a turning point in the entire religious, political, social, and economic history of the Province of Québec."

Trudeau made the decision after Asbestos that he had to teach and, hopefully, bring the brightest young minds in Québec to draw the same conclusions. He applied for a position at the Université de Montréal but found his effort stonewalled. It seemed that Duplessis himself had intervened to block him. Le Chef "didn't want any professors who had studied in a communist environment, in London and in Paris" teaching there, Trudeau later said. It seemed the 30-year-old had finally come to the conclusion that his training would serve Québec if he worked as a bureaucrat in government. Fate had other directions in store.

Trudeau moved to Ottawa, where a junior civil servant's position in the Privy Council Office (PCO) had been made available through an academic acquaintance. He looked upon the job offer as another learning experience that could further his understanding of the governmental process. "I wanted to observe in practice what I had just finished studying in theory," he said. The PCO needed Quebecers and was happy to welcome him because of his language and law training. Trudeau was given a desk in a garret of the East

Block and for the next two years served a civil service apprenticeship. As a French Canadian, he found the job humiliating. Civil servants from Québec functioned as a second-class tier in the mechanism of the federal bureaucracy. In code they referred to themselves as *"les Grecs"* because of the inferior treatment they received. Trudeau's evaluation of members of Parliament (MPs) from Québec was no less demeaning. He saw them as "trained donkeys" who worked at representation under the whips of their English-Canadian masters. By late 1951, he'd had enough. After all, he didn't need to work for the paycheque and felt he'd learned as much as he could in the PCO. The labour movement had offered him work and he took it gladly to return to Québec.

Several times a month he jumped on his motorcycle and went to cities across Québec, where he taught classes at labour action schools. He taught basic economics to several dozen militants brought together by the Confédération des travailleurs catholiques du Canada in each city. He helped negotiate collective agreements, meeting with judges appointed as arbitrators in labour disputes. Through the experience, he learned about the other end of the economic equation — workers and their rights.

The death of Le Chef in September 1959 created an instant opportunity for the Liberals to come to power. In June of the next year, under the leadership of Jean Lesage, the last vestiges of Duplessis' hold on Québec vanished. Without the premier's thumb holding them down, the Université de

Montréal was eager to offer Trudeau a position as head of an institute of public law. He still wanted to teach, however, so he joined the law faculty as professor of public law and declined the more administrative role as head of the institute.

Trudeau finally felt he was where he should be, and his intellectual energies were renewed. With Duplessis gone, he was seeing some of the transformation he'd witnessed in countries around the world now occurring in Québec. In the autumn of 1961 he began attending fortnightly meetings with other men just as passionate about discussing the reforms being undertaken. They included René Lévesque, a former Radio-Canada broadcaster; Trudeau's friend Gérard Pelletier, then the editor of *La Presse*; André Laurendeau, then the editor-in-chief of *Le Devoir*; and Jean Marchand, then the province's most influential labour leader. But while the group discussed how Québec might change, open itself even more to the world and free itself of insular politics, a new drum started beating an old rhythm in the province. It was the march to Québec nationhood. The Lesage government had opened the doors for what the press coined "the Quiet Revolution."

Québec entered an urgent phase of modernization. Its outlook became secular as opposed to religious. The traditionalism of the Duplessis period gave way to increasingly liberal attitudes. The province that had so often opposed change before the Lesage government now welcomed it. All of the values associated with the past were cut away except for one. Nationalism.

A greater role for the state was inevitable with the transformations that seemed to be required in Québec. Questioning the social order also led to a redefinition of the role and place of French Canadians in Canada. More people began calling for bilingualism, biculturalism, and the autonomy of Québec. The chant "*Le Québec aux Québécois*" began to be heard at political rallies. Increasingly, nationalism reflecting the collective goals of all Québec was being called for. And that gave impetus to a powerful separatist movement. Nationalism quickly became synonymous with the desire for social change.

The Liberals swept the province in another election in 1962 and René Lévesque, among the winning candidates, was called to the Cabinet. Lévesque was given the duty of nationalizing the private power companies in the province, consolidating them into a single company that had been planned in the 1940s under the Duplessis regime. Lévesque called it Hydro-Québec. The Liberals also set up a Ministry of Education to wrestle more control of schools from the Catholic Church. Lesage went after Ottawa for a larger slice of the national tax pie and the right for Québec to make its own foreign policy in relations with France. This encouraged the nationalists, who began demanding special constitutional status, perhaps even sovereignty. Feelings in Québec were being agitated by an increasing number of random bombings, the responsibility for which was claimed by a terrorist group calling themselves the Front de libération du Québec (FLQ).

For some time, Trudeau had privately worried about whether his days as a rebel were over. He wondered if rebellion would only mean driving his car too fast and growing his hair too long. And then he heard the nationalist's drum. Trudeau was suddenly energized by the prospect of fighting a new political enemy. In his eyes, Québec had thrown off the shackles of Duplessis and the Church only to wrap itself, almost immediately, in new chains of so-called nationalism. A separate Québec was folly, he thought. Only a strong process of federalism, with Québec as an equal partner in it, was acceptable in his opinion. He wanted to take action of some kind but could see no route until, in 1963, the Canadian electorate rejected a bickering Conservative Party led by John Diefenbaker and voted in a Liberal minority government under Lester Pearson.

Trudeau, working as editor of *Cité Libre*, a magazine he helped create to broadcast divergent political thought during the Duplessis period, focussed on putting his ideas about federalism across on paper. He avidly criticized the Québec Liberal experiment and saw them moving to the centre of the political spectrum, away from change. He also watched as, over the next two years, the federal Liberals tangled with the delicate balance of running a country without majority power.

Strategists in the Liberal machine worked relentlessly during the same period to find a way to attract stronger French support before their next test at the polls. The Québec caucus was pressing Jean Marchand to join their ranks, but he refused to go it alone. He was willing to run only if the party also welcomed Gérard Pelletier and another colleague. The third man was a law professor, perhaps too young for government at 45, but in Marchand's opinion eminently qualified. His name was Pierre Elliott Trudeau.

"These were the sort of men I was looking for; men of quality and standing in Québec, men who inspired both some admiration and some fear," Pearson later wrote. With the prime minister's blessing, the Liberal Party accepted Marchand's terms.

In September "The Three Wise Men" called a press conference at the Windsor Hotel in Montréal and announced they would run for Parliament. On November 8, 1965, each of them was elected.

Trudeau reacted to the victory with his patented response. He went to Europe for a brief ski holiday. While visiting his old LSE haunts in London early the next January, he fielded a call from the prime minister's office. Pearson was impressed with him and wanted the young lawyer turned MP as his parliamentary secretary. Pierre tried to duck. He told Pearson he wanted to go to Ottawa to present his ideas, not to seek power. He thought he needed time as an MP to do his "homework." He told the same thing to Marchand. Perhaps the wisest of the Three Wise Men, Marchand calmly told Trudeau to "grow up ... You said you wanted action! This is your chance."

Trudeau accepted the appointment, but tried to maintain a low profile in Ottawa. Socially he was hardly seen, preferring to live quietly in a suite at the Chateau Laurier. On weekends, and only in Montréal, he let his hair down for some flamboyant womanizing.

Until 1966, Trudeau's "I'm not really here" strategy had been working. He was finding his way around the parliamentary maze adeptly and performing his duties as parliamentary secretary without major problems. That June, however, Daniel Johnson took over the reins of Québec as premier. Johnson pulled no punches with Ottawa over his desire for the equality of complete independence for Québec. As part of his schema, he initiated diplomatic forays to France, seeking the support of France's president, Charles de Gaulle.

In Ottawa, Pearson was getting nervous about the international moves Johnson was making. He was well-acquainted with the art of international diplomacy and wanted to tightly monitor Johnson's foreign policy manoeuvres. The Liberals set up an informal committee and put Trudeau in place as its chairman. He was required to visit Paris officially, and in 1967 expanded his diplomatic work by travelling to Africa to assess Canada's relations with that continent's Francophone states. Trudeau had slipped into big league international political arenas almost seamlessly and Pearson was impressed.

From left to right, Pierre Trudeau, John Turner, Jean Chrétien, and then Prime Minister, Lester Pearson, in 1967

"No doubt Pearson felt I had a lot to learn about foreign policy. He was right. I knew the world at large fairly well, but I knew the world of diplomacy scarcely at all," Trudeau observed.

It took only 16 months after Trudeau was elected for him to be rewarded by Pearson yet again. In April 1967, the young politico became the minister of justice for Canada. While his friends couldn't be happier for him, his enemies were far less pleased with the Cabinet appointment. Conservative Opposition Leader John Diefenbaker was quick to point out Trudeau's lack of decorum. He criticized the clothes Trudeau sometimes wore to the House of Commons — leather sandals, slacks, and a sports coat. How could this egghead, this eccentric international gadfly, be a candidate for greatness? Diefenbaker saw only one side of Trudeau from his stodgy old-school point of view. But Trudeau could be Grace's good little boy one minute and Charlie's fighting grease monkey the next.

Trudeau met the challenge of his ministerial post with gusto and professionalism. As he worked diligently on pressing issues in the justice ministry, his charge, Daniel Johnson, was also working hard. Johnson had taken great pains to invite Charles de Gaulle to Québec in advance of the French president's official centennial visit to Ottawa and de Gaulle had accepted. On July 23, his cruiser, the *Colbert*, sailed up the St. Lawrence to Québec City. The next day de Gaulle rode in a triumphant cavalcade to Montréal.

The streets of Montréal were literally plugged with cheering French Canadians when de Gaulle disembarked from his limousine at noon onto the steps of Montréal City Hall. Evidently overcome by the patriotic response, de Gaulle agreed to make an impromptu speech to the thousands gathered there. He spoke of the spirit of liberation in France after World War II and the affection that modern France now held for "the French of Canada." Then he raised his arms and made the gesture of the victory "V" with his fingers.

"*Vive Montréal*," he said slowly, coaxing a roar from the crowd. "*Vive le Québec*," he said more loudly, and then basked in an even louder response from the crowd. Finally, turning to both sides first, he finally shouted the words that would place him forever in Canadian history and create a pivotal moment in the Québec nationalism crisis of the 1960s. "*Vive le Québec… libre!*" The crowd went wild.

With those four words, de Gaulle had managed to polarize Canada on the subject of Confederation and cause many deaf ears, in both English-speaking Canada and Québec, to hear Trudeau's siren call to federalism.

Chapter 5
Trudeaumania

ith a year of highly charged patriotism created by the Centennial and Expo 67 celebrations behind him, Lester Pearson decided to retire from politics.

Just before that December decision, Trudeau unveiled his Omnibus Bill to modernize Canadian divorce law and to amend the Criminal Code to liberalize laws against abortion and homosexuality. His Cabinet colleagues had needed some convincing, but they finally caved in to Trudeau's relentless arguments that government had no place determining what constituted sin for a generation of women flocking to the new mode of contraception provided by birth control pills.

"Well," the other ministers decided, "if you want to risk

destroying yourself, it's up to you." Trudeau told them he was prepared to take the political gamble. In his mind, the nation was ready for more liberalized views on marriage and sex. To a rapt national television audience, the soft-spoken minister with the Caesar-style haircut calmly justified his bill, saying, "the State has no place in the bedrooms of the nation." The catch phrase, lifted from an editorial by Martin O'Malley in the *Globe and Mail* newspaper, rang bells for Canadians. In the House of Commons it also sparked fierce debate, but the Omnibus Bill became law that month anyway.

Trudeau recalled the basic argument for the Omnibus Bill later in his life. "It was necessary first to prepare public opinion by drawing a very clear distinction between sin and crime. What is considered sinful in one of the great religions to which citizens belong isn't necessarily sinful in other religions. Criminal law therefore cannot be based on the notion of sin; it is crimes that it must define." The logic and cool manner with which he handled the furor impressed Pearson.

The prime minister was convinced the next leader of the Liberals had to be French Canadian if the Party was to maintain its grip on power in the future. He offered his tacit approval to Trudeau, should he decide to run for the leadership.

The MP from Outremont reacted to the offer of support with alarm. He was most concerned about what becoming the leader of the Liberals and the next Canadian prime minister would do to his personal freedom. He'd already seen how serving as the minister of justice claimed a huge chunk of his private life, and to Trudeau that element of privacy was sacrosanct. "You no longer belong to yourself," he said, pointing out that he thought it inappropriate for a new MP to seek the highest office in the land after barely two and a half years in Parliament and only nine months in Cabinet.

Pearson pressed further, however, as did Trudeau's closest friends, finally convincing him he had nothing to lose by putting his name forward in the leadership race. If he lost he'd still be an MP, but if he won he could create a new version of Canadian politics. And, they said, he could put his theories on federalism to the test. That carrot was too enticing for Trudeau to pass up. On February 16, 1968, he walked across the front lawn from the House of Commons to the National Press Club and declared himself.

Pearson insisted candidates continue performing their duties in the Legislature during the run-up to the leadership selection, which heavily restricted a candidate's ability to campaign. Because of his portfolio, however, Trudeau wasn't shackled in the same way. As the minister of justice, by mid-January he was already crisscrossing the country to every provincial capital to discuss Ottawa's reform proposals pending a constitutional conference of premiers to be held in early February. His face was in the news almost daily, and after his announcement, like a seasoned political veteran, he used every chance to promote his candidacy. When legitimate press opportunities didn't present themselves, he manufactured them. He was charming and debonair. After deliberately staging a pratfall down a flight of stairs and then bouncing up like an acrobat, he looked Canada in the eye and said, "I like to get fun out of life."

Trudeau was the precise opposite of what voters had been served up with their leaders in the past. No more stodgy old fatherly images. Here was a vital and comparatively young man with a sense of humour, a politician baby boomers could identify as one of their generation, a bachelor over whom women could literally swoon.

When Pearson opened the First Ministers' Constitutional Conference in Ottawa on February 5, there was only one man the nation was watching, Trudeau. Even Daniel Johnson succumbed. The nationalist Québec premier rejected outright the proposal for a new Charter of Rights being presented to the first ministers. Instead he turned the media spotlight over, saying the whole constitutional affair "was just Trudeau politicking." And he left the conference. It seemed that whatever happened in the six weeks leading up to the leadership convention, Trudeau was the one constant presence. He kept appearing front and centre.

When the selection was finally held, the Liberal gathering was more mob than convention. Party faithful of all ages seemed gripped by a curious fever. They wanted to be near him, to touch him. He was Canada's version of John F. Kennedy. Television cameramen and newspaper photographers couldn't get enough of his profile. Reporters wrote glowing articles about him. The Liberals' adoration was mystifying.

At the April 6 leadership convention, the seasoned old-guard candidates were drowned in the tidal wave of Trudeau's popularity. "The Trudeau campaign completely bewildered the old pros like Paul Martin, who could not understand the secret of its success," Pearson recalled. "As Paul said to me, 'How can someone who knows nothing of politics or the Party get so much support so suddenly, even from people like Joe Smallwood?' The answer was simple. Canadians thought of Paul Martin, or even of Paul Hellyer, in the context of Mackenzie King. They thought of Pierre Trudeau as a man for this season, uncontaminated and uninhibited." Even so, it took three ballots for Trudeau to assume the mantle of leadership.

The nation waited for the new prime minister to give them a taste of the future, but to everyone's consternation Trudeau was nowhere to be seen. The leadership campaign had been tiring, so Trudeau decided a vacation was in order. He disappeared. Though the Liberals and the country were waiting, watching, even expecting a hug after their tumultuous political lovemaking, he spirited his friend and political mentor Jean Marchand away for a two-week holiday. If Canadians didn't realize Trudeau did things his way by that simple gesture, they should have.

When Trudeau returned to Ottawa, everything was new. He took up residence at 24 Sussex Drive, the dwelling on a cliff overlooking the Ottawa River that became available to the head of government in 1955. It was probably a good thing it came with the job because going by his history, the new Canadian prime minister may otherwise have decided to live in a hotel room. Throughout his adult life, Trudeau had lived like a vagabond. The mansion in Ottawa was the first house of his own. While in Montréal he stayed with his mother and when travelling he had stayed in student digs or tiny rooms in the YMCA. Even as an MP, rather than make his home at a permanent address, he had lived at the Chateau Laurier Hotel. Not surprisingly, 24 Sussex Drive truly represented a sign of permanency for Trudeau. Even so, he arrived there with no more than a suitcase. He didn't know if his stay would be weeks, months, or years.

He explored his options. The question in his mind was whether he should attempt to govern with a minority so the Canadian people could get to know him or call a snap spring election while he was still hot news. And he was. During Pearson's mandate, only 15 people were required to handle the prime minister's correspondence but Trudeau's incoming mail was quadruple that amount. To deal with the flood, he soon had 60 people on his staff and he put his friend Marc Lalonde in charge of the PMO.

Trudeau polled his friends and the Liberal caucus for advice and overwhelmingly they told him to strike fast. On April 23, 1968, when the House reconvened, the nation learned what his answer was to be. On June 25, Canada would go to the polls. The nation's press had been expecting some kind of decision. A day before the House was to reconvene, they were camped outside his front door watching for a signal of Trudeau's intentions. The nimble new prime minister, however, showed them he was a target they had to watch, and even more, had to watch without blinking.

Using a hidden staircase from his office, Trudeau managed to slip by the press corps on Parliament Hill. At Rideau Hall, the residence of Governor General Roland Michener, he was just as sneaky. Rather than arrive as the press expected, if he was going to ask the governor general to dissolve Parliament, Trudeau approached unseen via a garden gate that was always closed. "I couldn't have the press announcing such important news before I did," he said with pesky delight.

The election campaign was a replay of his leadership battle. The adulation for him, which the press now coined "Trudeaumania," was immediately evident. Trudeau had seen the need to run for the leadership as an absolute imperative. The evil of Québec had to be fought.

He went to the people, telling them it was time justice was done in Canada. Twenty-seven percent of Canadians had French as their mother tongue and that had to be recognized. It was only just. The most disadvantaged had to be cared for by all Canadians. It was only just. Like his statements about keeping the nosy government out of their bedrooms, Trudeau coalesced his idea for Canadians in his speeches as the need for a "just society."

"Achieving such a society would require promoting equality of opportunity and giving the most help to those who were the most disadvantaged," he said. "Social security and equalization payments, as well as a ministry of regional economic expansion, would give practical effort to these abstract principles."

He ranged across the country with unending energy and Canadians, still in a festive mood after the success of the Centennial and Expo 67 in Montréal, responded in kind. If he wasn't speaking to crowds of thousands who were chanting his name, he was doing jack-knife dives into swimming pools or back flips on trampolines. Happily, he kissed every girl in sight on the campaign trail (Trudeau always hated kissing babies). He drew Canadians to his sparkling energy. This was perhaps most clearly evidenced in the staid surroundings of Victoria, British Columbia, a retirement enclave more British than Britain. Even there, the French-Canadian PM's popularity was phenomenal. To reach the microphones for his speech, Trudeau had to be lowered by helicopter because adoring fans had completely surrounded the hill where he was to speak.

By the time Trudeau took to the hustings, his inherent talent for debate was obvious. What had begun as wisecracks in class was now a razor-sharp ability honed by an incredible memory and clearly evident intelligence. For that reason he despised making speeches but relished opportunities to face

Pierre Trudeau signing autographs during his early years in power.

small groups or to banter one on one with voters. Hecklers were like candy to Trudeau on the campaign trail.

However, while his popularity was overwhelming in English-speaking Canada, Trudeau was only too aware of the separatist spectre still lurking in Québec. An active and vocal minority of separatists accused him of being a sell-out to their dreams of nationhood. The battle lines between them came to a noisy head the night before the election on June 28.

Saint-Jean-Baptiste Day is a day of celebration across Québec. It's a day of parades and parties to commemorate French-Canadian heritage. That month, Montréal Mayor Jean Drapeau had invited Trudeau to participate on the reviewing stand at that city's parade. Fearing that the festive event could turn into ugly demonstrations by separatists, Drapeau changed his mind 24 hours before the parade. He appealed to Trudeau to cancel his visit, but the prime minister rebuffed the request. "If you didn't want me to come, you shouldn't have invited me," he told the mayor. "Now that I've accepted, I'm certainly not going to admit, by backing down, that the prime minister of Canada can't watch the festival of Saint-Jean in his own home town! I've been watching this parade since I was six years old."

Trudeau arrived at the platform for dignitaries, in front of Montréal's municipal library, just as he said he would. He was flanked by Daniel Johnson and the archbishop of Montréal. For a time the celebrations were enjoyed by all, but a group of agitators, later identified as members of the Rassemblement pour l'indépendance nationale (RIN), began to thread their way through the parade as darkness fell over the celebrants. Before long they were running and throwing rocks and bottles towards the platform. The prime minister was not the only target, but he was obviously the preferred one. As the projectiles flew, near panic gripped the dignitaries and they rose, almost *en masse*, to leave. Despite the urgings of his Royal Canadian Mounted Police (RCMP) security, Trudeau refused to flee. Television cameras captured the moment with disturbing reality for the rest of Canada. There he was, the man they adored, resolutely facing a near riot of protesters and a hailstorm of debris. Alone. "I had absolutely no desire to give in to such a ridiculous display of violence," he said. "I detest violence."

The "night of stones" showed Canada that Trudeau was a man of courage. Stubborn, and perhaps even foolhardy in the face of such an obvious danger, but a prime minister unlike any before him.

The next day the nation responded. The Liberals won an overwhelming majority of 155 seats out of the 264 in the House of Commons. Trudeau had put an end to the string of minority governments in place in Canada since 1962.

Chapter 6
Just Watch Me

The efficiency of Parliament became an obsession for Trudeau. He immediately applied logical organization to the methods by which the Cabinet did business. Prior to his appearance, Cabinet meetings were known to be long, tedious sessions of argument and response as ill-prepared ministers tried to bring colleagues up to speed on the urgent needs in their portfolios. They met several times each week, sometimes even on Sundays, and their sessions could drag interminably into the early hours of the morning. "Inefficient," Trudeau said. "Start preparing memorandums."

The new prime minister insisted on knowing the intricate details of every ministry's business, and he told his ministers he couldn't possibly do that unless they were well apprised of their portfolios themselves. For the first time in Canadian history, Trudeau insisted each minister of the government take personal responsibility for the day-to-day business. "This is the fundamental discipline for the coherence of any government; all ministers must be responsible for all decisions made by the government of which they are a part," he said. Having been a minister, Trudeau knew how much more work that would put on each of his colleagues, but he adamantly stuck to his guns and the results were apparent immediately.

Cabinet under his leadership never met more than once a week on Thursdays and — except for very rare occasions — never sat for longer than four hours. The efficiency was necessary as Trudeau charged forward fulfilling his promise of reforms.

By October, he had created an Official Languages Act for Canada and the bureaucratic position of official languages commissioner. The Act asserted both French and English had to be spoken at federal institutions. Trudeau's legislation followed hard on the heels of the Royal Commission on Bilingualism and Biculturalism that Lester Pearson had established in 1963. The Royal Commission had recommended ways to heal the divide between Anglophones and Francophones. Trudeau began a round of appointments that inserted Quebecers in the government machine at Ottawa, which at that time was decidedly unilingual. The "French fact" had been ignored. As an example, Prime Minister Louis St. Laurent had been in office for several years before a plaque was put on his door identifying his office in French, his native tongue. If a Francophone civil servant wanted to write to another Francophone civil servant in Ottawa, the correspondence had to be done in English. When French Canadians visited Parliament, the parliamentary commissionaires who guided them often could not answer questions asked in French.

The Official Languages Act recognized that Canada had two languages and that both were equal before the law. It established the principle that every Canadian citizen has the right to communicate with federal authorities, institutions, and agencies in the official language of their choice. "The language of French Canadians was not being accorded equal treatment, a situation that could not be tolerated for long in the Just Society of which I dreamed," Trudeau said.

During his first term in office, Trudeau introduced metrication in Canada to bring the nation to what he felt were international standards. He introduced electoral reform. Prior to the election, political parties did not need to disclose their financial supporters. It left politicians open to special interest influence after they were elected. With Trudeau's reform, citizens were encouraged to support the political party of their choice and got the incentive of a tax deduction. All political contributions had to be disclosed. He moved Canada away from the Diefenbaker-inspired fiscal policy of pegging the Canadian dollar's value to that of the American greenback. Diefenbaker had pegged the dollar at 92.5 cents U.S. to guarantee Canadian manufacturers could be competitive with their American counterparts. Trudeau freed the dollar to float with other world currencies. He also created a task force to review each clause of the British North America Act. It was the first step in a plan Trudeau had for repatriating Canada's Constitution from Great Britain.

It seemed that Trudeau was driven to see change happen quickly, uncertain if he'd have the luxury of additional terms in office to introduce his legislation slowly. He became impatient with roadblocks, real or imagined. He'd always had a sarcastic side and it seemed to surface when he felt his vision was being questioned by anyone who failed to understand it. To put it bluntly, he didn't often feel his intellect was matched by his opponents. There were signs that the sweeping power voters had bestowed on the Liberals was going to Trudeau's head. His ego seemed inflated by the power he held. His normal air of superiority turned to arrogance. Political pundits in the press were reviled for their failure to agree with his policies. He even took to insulting them publicly, calling them "a crummy lot."

In the House of Commons, the shift in his attitude from the fun-loving young prime minister to his more pedantic intellectual side was quite apparent. Trudeau had little respect for most Conservative opposition MPs. Though he never stooped to assassinations of an individual's character, he was only too willing to denigrate them as a group.

On one occasion, as Trudeau tried to manoeuvre the business to a close for a holiday, the Tory opposition was obstinately demanding the House remain in session to continue debate. Trudeau reacted with sarcasm. The Tories appealed to the Speaker of House, claiming that by his statements, the prime minister showed no respect for the elected representatives of the people. "When they get home, when they get out of Parliament, when they are 50 yards from Parliament Hill, they are no longer honorable members — they are just nobodies, Mr. Speaker," Trudeau replied. His "nobodies" comment reinforced the impression the Canadian electorate was forming. The media, delighted to get back at Trudeau for his mean-spirited description of them, carried the quote in bold headlines across the country. Trudeau's staff responded by asking the nation to cut him slack. Re-making Canada is a big job, they said, and he has a lot on his mind. Canada didn't have to be told. It already knew.

Québec continued to be a thorn in the side of those who backed a strong federal government. "Sovereignty-association" supporters, led by René Lévesque, said the other nine provinces of Canada were working towards greater centralization of authority. For Québec to assert autonomy, Lévesque argued that Québec had to become a nation-state that contracted with the rest of Canada in areas of mutual interest. Radical separatists called for an independent nation again. Trudeau still equated the efforts for Québec nationalism with the spirit of Duplessis and the conservative Catholicism he'd been battling since the 1940s. "I entered politics with my friends to prove that French Canadians are as good as anyone else; they have no need to be ghettoized by special status or a two-nations theory," he said.

The radical separatists, however, had been steadily increasing their violent assaults since 1963. By 1969, more than 200 violent crimes, including 60 bombing incidents, had been recorded. More bombing occurred that year, in fact, than in the five previous years combined. One blast at the Montréal Stock Exchange had injured 27 people.

In response, a new committee of Cabinet had been formed by Trudeau to deliberate the problems of public security generally, and in particular those being created by the FLQ. At a December 1969 meeting of that committee, Trudeau called upon those responsible in the RCMP to "gather information on the sources of financing for the separatist movement in Québec, the public service, political parties, universities, unions and professions, and on the political troubles in Québec."

Trudeau said he had two things in mind when making that request. First, he wanted to know more about terrorist activity. Secondly, he wanted the functionaries in the RCMP to become more familiar with the nature of separatism and the root causes for a group that sought the dissolution of Canada. He thought that, until that time, the RCMP had only focussed on threats from outside ideologies such as communism. The people advocating violent separation in Québec could come from good, middle-class families and he wanted the RCMP to realize and understand the distinction.

In reviewing the request he had made of the RCMP, Trudeau didn't think it necessary to explain that he didn't mean for the police to investigate legitimate democratic opposition parties. But, without that clarification, the RCMP took a different view of his request. They began to search for more than bombings and bank robberies committed to finance FLQ violence. Their interest went deeper, searching for the evil of terrorism in every activity of the Parti Québecois. They viewed writers and the press with suspicion. Inadvertently, by not being assiduous in his terms, Trudeau had created a serious breach of trust with the Canadian people. It would take years of explaining in the future to resolve, because the RCMP believed they had been asked to spy on their own citizens. "The Mounties had the right, and even the duty, to keep track of anyone they suspected of treason, even if such suspects were members of a democratic party. But they ought not to have targeted the party as a whole," he said later about the Parti Québecois spying.

The fallout from his request became clear with the arrests made in October 1970. By then, 23 members of the FLQ were serving jail sentences, including four convicted for murders. On February 26, 1971, the police arrested two men who were driving a panel truck that contained a sawed-off shotgun and a communiqué announcing the kidnap of the Israeli consul. One of the men was Jacques Lanctôt. That capture was followed by a June police raid on a home in Prévost, a community in the Laurentian Mountains north of Montréal. There, the police discovered 136 kilograms of dynamite, ammunition, detonators, and the draft of a ransom note that was to have been used in the planned kidnapping of the United States consul.

It was obvious the Québec nationalism issue was dangerously hot. The FLQ terrorists had warned of more bombings in their official communication organ, *La Cognée*. They were clearly in pursuit of the violent destruction of the Canadian federation, reflecting a trend by Quebecers who felt they were prisoners in Canada. A report compiled at the Université de Montréal in the mid-1960s claimed that 38 percent of that city's residents lived in poverty or privation. There was real and justifiable distrust for the system simmering there.

On October 5, 1970, James Cross, the British trade commissioner stationed in Montréal, was kidnapped from his home on Redpath Crescent by the Liberation cell of the FLQ. His captors made the following demands: the release of 23 "political prisoners"; $500,000 in gold; the broadcast and publication of the FLQ manifesto; the publication of the names of the police informants for terrorist activities; an aircraft to take the kidnappers to Cuba or Algeria; the cessation of all police search activities; and the rehiring of the Lapalm truck drivers who had lost their jobs when their company lost its contract with the post office. The Manifesto called the truckers "*gars de Lapalm*" and said they were victims of a heartless capitalist federal system. The truckers had travelled to Ottawa to protest their lost jobs, only to be met by a taunt from Trudeau, who had told them, "*Mange de la merde*," which, when colloquially translated, means "eat shit".

Nothing like the October Crisis had ever happened in Canadian history. "The sheer senselessness of it caught us off guard," Trudeau said, "which meant we were badly equipped to deal with it." Within two days, 30 people were arrested in police raids. Mitchell Sharp, as secretary of state for external affairs, was forced to handle the crisis since James Cross was a diplomat and Canada was responsible for guaranteeing his safety. As the Cabinet deliberated over the FLQ, with Trudeau unwilling "to give them [the FLQ] an inch," Sharp tried to buy time for the RCMP investigations. He authorized the reading of the terrorist manifesto over the CBC's Radio-Canada on October 8, 1970.

On October 10, less than a week after Cross disappeared, the FLQ launched a second assault on Canada's sensibility. Pierre Laporte, the vice premier of Québec and minister of labour, was also kidnapped. This time the crime was committed in broad daylight, from the front of his South Shore home, by the Chenier cell of the FLQ. Within hours of the second kidnapping, Premier Bourassa made a desperate telephone call to Trudeau. "Pierre, you are going to have to send in the army, and you should think about invoking the War Measures Act (WMA)," he said. Bourassa was concerned about the inflamed situation. Angry crowds were gathering in Montréal, defiantly shouting "*Vive le FLQ*." Bourassa feared outright civil insurrection.

Trudeau showed calm leadership. Invoking the War Measures Act meant suspending civil liberties completely. The WMA was the only means at the federal government's disposal for declaring a state of emergency. "The consequences of such a measure would be extremely serious, and we have no proof that it is necessary. I prefer not to think about it," the prime minister said. Trudeau agreed to send the army "in aid of the Civil Power" if the provincial government made a formal request, and the RCMP kept him abreast of the crisis with hourly reports. Soon he learned that Bourassa had received a letter written by Laporte in which the politician pleaded for his life. Responding to the urgent needs expressed by one of their own, the Québec Cabinet attempted to negotiate with the terrorists, but those talks quickly broke down.

To protect the House of Commons, Trudeau decided to dispatch the army to guard Ottawa on October 12. When he was questioned on the steps of the Legislature the next day he responded softly, "I think the society must take every means at its disposal to defend itself against the emergence of a parallel power which defies the elected power in this country." The CBC's Tim Ralfe then posed a question, the answer to which Canadians would never forget. "Just how far would you go?" Ralfe asked. "Just watch me," Trudeau answered.

On October 14, Trudeau called a special Cabinet meeting to discuss what to do about the abductions and the FLQ's demands. He could see that the situation in Québec was spinning out of control. The following day, a group of respected business and government leaders in Québec, including René Lévesque, head of the Parti Québécois, and Claude Ryan, the editor of *Le Devoir*, along with 14 others, called for the Québec government to negotiate with the terrorists. Bourassa broached the Québec National Assembly with a different plan. He received the full support of his government and all three opposition parties to call on the services of the army under the National Defense Act. In total, 7500 troops (including those already in Ottawa) were quickly deployed to Montréal and Québec City.

In the early morning of October 16, after Bourassa officially asked Ottawa to declare a state of "apprehended insurrection" and to impose martial law in Québec, Trudeau knew he could no longer vacillate. He imposed the War Measures Act at 4:00 a.m. It was the only occasion when it had been imposed in peacetime (it had previously been imposed during the two world wars).

The boy who had stared down street toughs on rue Durocher, the man who faced flying bottles and stones in Montréal seemingly unafraid, was spoiling for a fight. Within hours the army and police swooped across the province and arrested more than 250 Québec residents who were suspected of being communist supporters or FLQ sympathizers. They were held for questioning without charges or trial. Before the arrests were over, 247 more people were taken, including labour leaders, entertainers, writers, and members of the Parti Québécois. Many were held for days, unable to contact a lawyer and subjected to what the Québec Civil Liberties Union later described as "absolutely unacceptable" questioning techniques. Of all those arrested, only 62 were actually charged.

Unfortunately, the Chenier cell responded in kind. On October 17, they announced they had executed their hostage, Pierre Laporte. The FLQ told the police they could find his body in the trunk of a car that was abandoned near Saint-Hubert Airport, a few kilometers from Montréal. The communiqué derisively referred to the politician as the "minister of unemployment and assimilation." When the police recovered Laporte's body, they found he had been strangled by the gold chain of his own crucifix. "To lose an old friend, and in such a manner, just when we were trying to come to his aid, to come face to face with the inhuman cruelty of these anonymous assassins, was atrocious," Trudeau said.

After the wave of arrests, Trudeau offered his regrets about the number of innocents swept up in the police nets. "Naturally, I would prefer that it hadn't taken place, that the FLQ had never seen the light of day, and that Pierre Laporte were still among us. But wishes do not change reality." Opinion polls showed that most of Canada agreed with him.

Immediately following the announcement of Laporte's murder, the Liberation cell declared that James Cross would also be murdered if their demands were not met or if the "fascist police" discovered their whereabouts. It took three tense weeks, during which Canadian soldiers patrolled Québec streets, before a police raid uncovered the Chenier cell's hiding place. Three FLQ members escaped but Bernard Lortie was arrested and charged with the kidnapping and murder of Laporte. Lortie's capture, however, didn't break the back of the Liberation cell. The clock continued to tick and the police found themselves hopelessly unable to find him despite a house-to-house search. Time, they feared, was not on their side. Police finally crumpled to the Liberation cell's demands out of desperation and negotiated with the kidnappers. It was a last resort, but one that everyone felt was required before Cross followed the tragic example the Chenier cell had made with Laporte. On December 3 — 60 days after he'd been kidnapped and imprisoned in an 8 by 12 foot room on des Récollets Street in Montréal North — James Cross was released by the Liberation cell.

At the same time that Cross gained freedom, five known members of the terrorist cell were granted safe passage to Cuba aboard a Canadian Forces aircraft. One of them was Jacques Lanctôt. The five terrorists were later found to be living in Paris, France. Two days after Christmas, the three remaining members of the Chenier cell were captured in St. Luc after police found them hiding in a six-metre tunnel. Paul Rose, Jacques Rose, and Francis Simard were all charged. Paul Rose, the leader of the Chenier cell, had first become involved with the Québec nationalist group in 1968. He had met Jacques Lanctôt during Trudeau's "night of stones," the near-riot at the Saint-Jean-Baptiste parade.

On March 31, 1971, he and Paul Simard were sentenced to life imprisonment for the murder of Pierre Laporte. Bernard Lortie received a 20-year sentence in jail for kidnapping. Paul Rose was granted full parole on December 20, 1982. A report in 1980 revealed he was not actually present when Laporte was murdered. Jacques Rose was acquitted of both the murder and kidnapping but later he was found guilty of being an accessory after the fact and sentenced to eight years in jail. He was paroled in July 1978.

Over the years, all of the exiled Liberation cell members returned to Canada to face trial. They were convicted of kidnapping and sentenced to jail terms that ranged from 20 months to two years. In July 1980, a sixth person, Nigel Barry Hamer, was arrested in connection with the Cross kidnapping. He pleaded guilty and was sentenced to 12 months in jail as well.

Pierre Trudeau slowly began to relax once Cross was released. The FLQ trauma for Canada had been overcome, but he knew the spectre of Québec separatism still lurked in the body of federalism, like a disease in remission. The crisis weeks had changed him, strengthened his resolve. "What the October Crisis taught me," he wrote, "was that it is absolutely essential to have, at the helm of state, a very firm hand, one that sets a course that never falters, that does not attempt to do everything at once out of excitement or confusion, but that moves along slowly, step by step, putting solutions in place."

Trudeau believed he knew the solution to the Québec question. It was now just a matter of getting there.

Chapter 7
Enter the Flower Child

She was 19 years old and he was 48, more than twice her age, but that didn't matter much to either of them. Under the hot South Pacific sun, where inhibitions are so often discarded, friendships come easily. That's how it was for them in December 1967 on the Island of Tahiti.

Trudeau had just been asked to reach for the brass ring in Ottawa and was taking time to relax at an all-inclusive tropical resort while he decided if he was up to the task. To fill time, the young federal justice minister was wowing sunbathers on the beach with his water-skiing skill. When he came back to dry land, Margaret offered a compliment. She rarely had trouble striking up conversations with strangers.

Her easy smile and attractive figure were usually more than enough reason for any male nearby to take notice. That included Pierre, who enjoyed flirting as much as the next man.

They relaxed by the water and chatted idly, ranging over subjects from Plato to rebellion. Margaret was not terribly excited by his company. He was old enough to be her father. But he did have a youthful attitude, and that intrigued her. To kill the boredom of sunbathing all the time, she agreed to join him for some deep-sea fishing a few days later. After three hours of chatting, she wandered over to where her mother was sitting. Kathleen Sinclair had been watching the scene. She was almost the same age as the man Margaret had met. Wife of James Sinclair, former Liberal fisheries minister in the Louis St. Laurent government, she'd been a widow to politics for years. When her daughter approached, she asked if Margaret realized with whom she'd been speaking. "Oh, Pierre someone or other," Margaret replied. Not just any Pierre, her mother said. That Pierre was the minister of justice. It didn't impress Margaret. In fact, knowing the truth actually made her less interested. She'd had her fill of politicians at an early age and immediately decided to blow off their fishing date. "I was young and romantic; Pierre struck me as very old and very square," Margaret later recalled in her autobiography.

Trudeau was completely immersed in his battle for the leadership when he met Margaret again during the Liberal

Margaret Sinclair Trudeau

Convention in 1968. In 1969, using the perks of his position, he managed to privately convey his desire to see her again on a date in her hometown of Vancouver. He hadn't forgotten her, even though he'd briefly dated singer Barbra Streisand and Canadian actress Margot Kidder.

In the 18 months since he'd seen her last, Margaret had graduated and gained some world experience in travel. She'd also fulfilled the image of a free spirit of the 1970s, experimenting extensively with drugs and sex both in Vancouver and Morocco, where she'd gone after her graduation. Her attitude towards men, particularly Trudeau, had also changed. The coolness she'd shown after learning who he was in Tahiti quickly vaporized when he became the most powerful man in Canada. She'd seen the adoration held by women across the country for this trim erudite Don Juan, and a passionate romance quickly blossomed between the two.

Margaret was of Scottish heritage, like Trudeau's mother Grace. She was young, witty, and sexy. She was the quintessential earth mother and a lover of dancing, poetry, and evidently Pierre. Being with her was a boost to his 50-year-old self-esteem, and it also enhanced his image as a non-conformist. It was a story that had repeated itself time and again through history — an older, wealthy and worldly man attracts a youthful woman intoxicated by his power. They maintained a deepening relationship for months in total secrecy. With the help of her father's contacts, Margaret secured herself a six-month job in Ottawa so the couple was able to see each other more frequently. Often that amounted to romantic weekend trysts at the prime minister's country residence at Harrington Lake.

It was apparent to Trudeau's friends that the affection was flowing both ways. For too long he'd been the lonely bachelor, and he confessed to them that he thought he was in love with Margaret. Some of his peers thought she had bedazzled him. When he decided to present Margaret to his dying mother, bedridden with arteriosclerosis and only occasionally lucid, they knew the relationship was serious. Trudeau asked Margaret to marry him and during the engagement, his young bride-to-be returned to Vancouver in order to convert to Catholicism.

On March 4, 1971, Canada was introduced to the new Mrs. Trudeau after a small private wedding in Vancouver. Stunning in the wedding gown she had made for herself, the nation feasted on the scant few photographs that were allowed during the wedding ceremony. The couple was pictured taking their vows and cutting the wedding cake she had baked. Overnight, the 23-year-old woman became a national celebrity and she basked in the attention. The marriage seemed a fairy tale come true. Their first child, Justin, was born on Christmas Day, 1971. It was the first birth to a sitting Canadian prime minister in 102 years. Outwardly, Margaret appeared as though she were still living the honeymoon.

For Trudeau, a honeymoon of another kind was already over. When he'd assumed office, Canada was in the midst of a period of exceptional growth that had lasted since 1962. But as Canada entered 1972, Trudeau found his public support seriously declining. Trudeau, the Cabinet, and External

Affairs Minister Mitchell Sharp had determined that Canada had to reduce its dependence on the United States. They took forceful steps to strengthen Canadian ownership of the economy, to protect Canadian culture, and to diversify Canada's trade abroad. Canadian business reacted fearfully, worried about an American backlash at the border. But Trudeau was grounded firmly in his belief that such action was necessary before his country slid further beneath America's industrial thumb.

As well as the Official Languages Act, Trudeau's Liberals had achieved the diplomatic recognition of mainland China and the Vatican, lowered the age of majority from 21 to 18 years, and revamped the functions in Parliament. Across the nation, however, the electorate was grumbling. Trudeau, voters said, didn't care about ordinary citizens' concerns about unemployment and inflation. In the year previous, the United States president, Richard Nixon, had faced major economic headaches with a recession, and had arbitrarily imposed a 10 percent surcharge on all goods entering the United States. Since the U.S. was Canada's largest trading partner, this had a negative impact on Canada's economy.

Trudeau continued to push through more reforms during the second two years of his mandate, despite the grumbling of the nation. The Liberals set up the Canada Development Corporation to help build a higher Canadian stake in the nation's key industries. They formed Canada's first Ministry of Environment and undertook the colossal task, with Ontario, of cleaning up Lake Erie. They introduced maternity benefits through unemployment insurance, voted in a capital gains tax, and created a youth employment program.

Trudeau felt his government could stand on its record when he called an election for October 1972. Then, ignoring the advice of the Liberal Party election machine, he tried to distance himself from the emotionalism of Trudeaumania. Late in the election, he realized his strategy was wrong. "The approach was too cerebral. Politics can't be conducted at such a rational level, devoid of all emotion. The voters wanted a leader to guide them, and I was giving them a professor," he observed. He thought Canadians should vote with their heads. But Canadians vote with their hearts first.

Trudeau's reputation as a reformer was tainted. The New Democratic Party (NDP) leader, David Lewis, attacked the record being held up to scrutiny, claiming the government had been too timid with tax reform. He denounced the nation's "corporate welfare bums" who were receiving huge subsidies from Ottawa without providing guarantees to hire more workers in return.

The result of Trudeau's strategy showed in the tally of votes after the polls closed on October 22. The Liberals lost their majority and squeaked into power with only a two-seat edge over Robert Stanfield's Conservatives. For the next 20 months, Trudeau led a tenuous minority government, only in power with the brokered support of the NDP. He walked a tightrope but his government still managed to introduce social legislation that enhanced the lives of Canada's less-advantaged. The government introduced the indexing of old age pension and higher unemployment insurance benefits. Trudeau's Liberals also created the Foreign Investment Review Agency.

In 1974, Trudeau had had enough of minority government anxiety. Using a federal budget he knew would not be supported by either the Conservatives or the NDP, he engineered a non-confidence vote in the House to force another election. When the Liberals went to the voters in 1974, the Canadian economic picture was a disaster. Inflation was practically runaway and, curiously, unemployment was rapidly growing at the same time. Trudeau's fiscal policies had let the money supply grow in Canada.

When the Organization of Petroleum Exporting Countries (OPEC) decided on a ten-fold increase in the price of petroleum exports in the wake of the 1973 Arab–Israeli Yom Kippur War, inflation climbed over 10 percent. Trudeau reacted by establishing a Canada-wide, one-price policy that set the Canadian price of crude below the world price. Americans owned 28 percent of Canada's petroleum industry. Trudeau feared the United States would use that position to drain Canada's reserves for cheaper oil. To combat that risk, he applied an oil export tax. He also acted to have the Interprovincial Pipeline extended from Sarnia, Ontario, to Montréal, and he established a national oil company, Petro-Canada.

Economists had no experience in dealing with the problem of inflation and unemployment rising simultaneously. What was considered a remedy for inflation was precisely the opposite of the remedy for unemployment. A new term was added to the economic lexicon— stagflation. When Trudeau went back to the voters a second time, he had learned his lesson about listening to his political advisors in the Liberal party. They told him he had to resurrect his Trudeaumania image if he could, perhaps this time relying on a new look, that of a family man instead of a playboy.

Margaret, who'd given birth to their second son, Alexander (Sacha), on Christmas Day 1973, agreed to fight at her husband's side. It was the first and only time she did so. Having her along on the campaign trail cramped Trudeau's style. Before that, he'd always been able to separate his lives into two parts, public and private. With Margaret tag-teaming, Trudeau could never drop the mask of politics at the end of the day and just be Pierre. The imbalance disturbed him, as he was intensely protective of his privacy. Trudeau felt that the nation's scrutiny of his private life, with Margaret always at his side, somehow stole his freedom. Since his youth, he'd been a loner. Even on camping expeditions he would lead on the trail so he could be alone. If his companions caught up with him, he'd slacken his pace and purposely fall far behind them for the same reason. Privacy was in his nature.

But Margaret's assistance with the campaign was working with the voters. The press enjoyed photographing her and the nation loved seeing the pictures. On the election trail, the attention was deflected to her, allowing Trudeau to concentrate on politics. And he was overjoyed by Robert Stanfield's platform. The Conservative leader espoused a state-enforced wage and price freeze as the solution to rampant inflation and rising unemployment. He wanted to follow these with a period of wage and price controls on the national economy. Trudeau told the nation that the price of goods in Canada was determined outside the country. "He's going to control your wages," he warned voters, "not prices."

Partly on the basis of his criticisms of Stanfield's plan, Trudeau once again returned to Ottawa with a majority government and promptly rolled up his sleeves. He was ready to take on a fight with the economy, but didn't yet realize he had another battle as well, on the home front.

Margaret had enjoyed the limelight beside Trudeau during the election, even giving some speeches herself on his behalf. The day after the votes were counted, however, life returned to its stifling pre-election normalcy at 24 Sussex. Trudeau spent most of his time away and when at home, was buried in his office behind high stacks of paper. He may have been a brilliant politician, but as a father he still had much to learn. Margaret, still immature, didn't know how to deal with the transition back to reality. The seven weeks on the election trail had been the best weeks in her married life and suddenly they were over. She was later to confess to a writer, "something in me broke that day." To another reporter she described what happened to her as a fantasy. "It was a fairy tale at the beginning of our marriage and our relationship. It was bliss, just bliss. But I was very young and had a lot of growing to do. The world was not a place for fairy tales. Fairy tales don't happen, real life happens."

The couple were so drastically different. Compatibility became an issue as romance began to fade. Margaret later admitted she was not Trudeau's match intellectually. "Culture to me," she said, "was rock music." Margaret had trouble discussing matters that interested Trudeau and didn't try. On the other hand, either he was inflexible and made no effort to find common ground or he demeaned her for her lack of knowledge. A sad example was once recounted by family friends who were perplexed by Trudeau's behaviour when he deliberately excluded Margaret from their dinner conversation. "Don't worry about her," he told them. "She wouldn't know what we were saying, even if we were speaking English."

Trudeau was a self-contained soul. During their time together, as far as he was concerned, if the marriage needed adjustments, they would have to be made by Margaret. At that time, she was simply incapable of the task. To fight her boredom, she took to quarrelling with the household staff, going on spending sprees for extravagant clothes, and home decorating. She also entered into open combat for Trudeau's attention. She left home without consultation on solitary holidays and sought to fill the void she felt with an illicit affair.

She began to smoke a significant amount of marijuana at home. “It became so that Pierre, on arriving home from the office, would come up not to kiss but to sniff me,” she said.

The distractions only delayed the inevitable breakdown of her health. In September, just two months after the election, she threatened to kill herself with a kitchen knife. The suicide threat came after an encounter with Trudeau when he confronted her over rumours that she'd been romantically involved with Edward Kennedy at a celebrity tennis match in New York. That night, the prime minister's 26-year-old wife was admitted to Montréal General Hospital, suffering from severe emotional stress.

For Margaret, at least it was a break from that “large cold grey mansion” on Sussex Drive.

Chapter 8
Eating His Words

Faced with two crises in his life in 1975, Trudeau's ability to separate home and office was failing. On the job in Ottawa, his marriage problems haunted him. Margaret was released from the hospital and had begun a series of psychiatric consultations. He encouraged her to apply her energies to something he considered productive and she decided to attempt photography, taking lessons to become a professional. Trudeau was adamant that he had never lost any real battle in his life and he was not about to lose her if he could help it. He said he realized that he'd been learning about parenting at the same time as he was learning about politics. He later observed, "Perhaps it was a little too much for me and, regrettably, I didn't succeed all that well."

On September 2, Trudeau cradled his third son, Michel, in his arms and gave himself over completely to family. But it was short lived. Canada needed his guidance just as desperately.

Inflation had leaped to an annual rate of 10.8 percent and there was danger of it going out of control. While unemployment had modestly decreased, it hung with seven percent of the national workforce out of work. Appeals for a "tripartite" direction for the economy — major companies, unions, and government working together to set and implement economic targets — had failed. Trudeau struggled with finding a remedy. Both he and Finance Minister John Turner had been identified as the chief critics of Robert Stanfield's policy solutions during the election campaign. Trudeau wanted to avoid being accused of adopting the Tory answer, that is, wage and price controls. The pressure was getting to Turner, who thought there was no other solution to the economic morass in which Canada found itself. On September 10, the popular minister resigned, citing fatigue and a need to spend more time with his family. The resignation only heightened the atmosphere of crisis, and Trudeau faced a belligerent press wanting answers to questions about his economic remedies. He had to stand alone. He searched his caucus for a replacement for Turner and latched on to Donald Macdonald, an able politician he knew who was also against wage and price controls. However, once Macdonald had taken over the finance portfolio, Trudeau heard the same litany. Canada had no choice.

On Thanksgiving Day, Trudeau took television time from the CBC and announced the creation of the Anti-Inflation Board (AIB) and the institution of wage and price controls for a three-year period. Trudeau said the federal government would be the first to take the bitter medicine and clamped freezes on spending and wages in the civil service, hoping the example would be followed by business and labour. It was. Inflation began to drop (by 1976 it slid to 7.5 percent and in 1977 it hovered at about 7.9 percent). In hindsight, other economic experts said the controls actually hurt the economy. The Conference Board of Canada, a research organization sponsored by large companies, later claimed that "controls resulted in a significant shift in income distribution in Canada away from persons and in favour of business" compared to what it felt should have occurred from 1975 to 1978, had the program not been introduced. Government spending was also digging Canada deeper into debt. In 1975 the national deficit was $3.8 billion and it was projected to be $10.9 billion by 1978. Trudeau downplayed the long-term effect of an increasing deficit. The face of national politics was changing, and he felt that the economic crisis seemed under better control with the restriction. He had to deal with the matter of national unity just as urgently.

In 1976, the Progressive Conservatives had opted for leadership youth, too, and chose gentlemanly Joe Clark as a replacement for Robert Stanfield. In Québec, Réne Lévesque and his Parti Québécois gained power in that province's National Assembly as well. The prime minister looked favourably on the news from Québec. Lévesque had campaigned on a separatist platform in 1970, which saw only seven people elected, garnering just 23 percent of the popular vote. In 1973, he tried again, but only saw six people elected with a marginal improvement to 30 percent of the popular vote. Trudeau used those facts to claim separatism was dead in Québec. But, likely, he knew in his heart the dragon was, at best, only dying. He believed he had to get the Constitution repatriated to heal the wounds of separatism, but just as realistically, he admitted getting Québec's support was an impossibility. "When you look at the matter coldly, it's clear that there never was a realistic chance of persuading a separatist party to renew the Constitution of Canada. They were in politics to break up Canada, not preserve it."

Unanimous consent from all the provinces was a pipe dream as well. Though Trudeau consistently tried to bring them together on the Constitution at annual premiers' conferences, the premiers of the other provinces were using Lévesque as foil for demands of their own. They ransomed their support of a renewed Constitution with demands for everything from jurisdiction of cable television in their provinces to the control of the fisheries. Results of the premiers' conferences showed an ever-growing list of demands each time they sat down. Trudeau decided that perhaps to reach his dream of a nation with its own constitution, he would have to prepare the Canadian people for a break from convention. Perhaps the federal government would simply have to make an appeal to London for its constitutional independence without unanimous provincial consent.

His efforts at building bridges of understanding on the home front were no better. Over the next three years his marriage continued to falter. Finally, in March 1977, he and Margaret decided on a trial separation. He would retain custody of the boys while she used the time to explore a new life apart from him. She did so with a vengeance, joining the high-flying jet set, and the media feasted on her shenanigans. They watched as she danced the night away in exclusive nightclubs and partook in backstage parties with rock musicians. For Trudeau, his wife's assaults on his Catholic morals, and the criticism of his leadership from every corner of Canada, seemed relentless. In 1978 it was clear, even to him, that Canadians were alienated. In the West his popularity was at an all-time low.

By 1978, Canadian oil prices had been raised to world levels and the federal government had reached an agreement with Alberta on resource sharing. With Ontario, Alberta and Ottawa were also working together to save the development of the Syncrude Tar Sands Oil Project. Then the roof caved in on oil prices a second time. When Mohammed Rez Pahlavi was ousted from power as the Shah of Iran, that country stopped producing oil. Virtually overnight the world price shot from $14US to over $34US a barrel. Economists predicted it could climb to as much as $100 a barrel. The resource-sharing agreement Trudeau had worked out with Alberta saw the feds receiving 9 percent of oil and gas revenues, the producing provinces 50.5 percent, and industry 40.5 percent. Trudeau was suddenly alarmed. If prices continued to rise "Canada wouldn't even have been able to continue its equalization program. Even Ontario would have become a have-not province" under the formula. In October 1980, with Marc Lalonde as energy minister, the Liberals announced the National Energy Program (NEP) as part of the federal budget. It envisaged Canadianization of the largely foreign-owned energy industry.

The oil and gas sector accounted for about 50 percent of all the income generated in Alberta at that time. Oil production had been providing over half the Alberta budget since the late 1960s. Trudeau said the OPEC price hikes had induced windfall profits in Alberta, and that it was something all Canadians should share. With the NEP, Ottawa introduced new taxes at the wellhead, and called for 50 percent Canadian ownership in the oil and gas sector. Alberta Premier Peter Lougheed was livid. "The Ottawa government — without negotiation and without agreement — simply walked into our homes and occupied the living room."

Trudeau wanted to keep domestic oil prices below world prices so that eastern manufacturers would have a competitive advantage. Alberta, with little to no manufacturing capability, saw it as a "cash grab" on oil income. The NEP generated an immediate panic in the exploration industry. American investment flew south and Alberta's oil and gas exploration, and its service and supply sectors, tanked. Incentives in the NEP for Canadian companies willing to explore in remote regions like the Beaufort Sea did nothing for drilling contractors or small supply companies south of Edmonton. Businesses closed. Jobs were lost. Albertans also began calling for separation. Foreign control of the industry fell from 37 percent in 1971 before the NEP to 23.6 percent in 1986 after it, and American ownership fell from 28 percent to 17 percent.

Alberta reacted with more than verbal outrage, however. The province reduced the flow of oil to the other provinces by 180,000 barrels a day, forcing Ottawa to compensate by buying more expensive foreign oil. The cost advantage Trudeau was after for eastern manufacturers backfired. Trudeau's team went into tough bargaining mode with Alberta right away. In September 1981, a compromise on revenues acceptable to all sides was reached. The federal share of oil revenues would go up to 26 percent while the Alberta and industry shares would decline to 37 percent. The compromise would have been fine if oil prices had continued to rise, but soon after the deal was inked prices stabilized and started to fall even as interest rates skyrocketed.

That summer, the U.S. Federal Reserve Board allowed interest rates to rise to record levels to combat higher oil prices. The world economy, tied to the United States, had to do it too. By August 1981, a month before the new revenue-sharing formula was signed, the Bank of Canada had been forced to raise its rates from 7.5 percent to 21 percent. For Albertans, it was a double whammy. People were out of work, without prospects, and walking away from their mortgaged homes. The word Liberal would be spelled with four letters for a very long time.

Trudeau, however, was not apologetic for his attempts to create more equal resource sharing and a homegrown energy policy. His attitude towards governing was now braced by the conclusions he'd reached after the FLQ crisis. A good leader was strong and abided by his principles.

Trudeau had not applied much effort to foreign policy and now resolved that had to change as well. Though his initiatives for trade agreements with Moscow had been credited as the beginnings of East-West détente, he'd not taken bold steps on the world stage. He realized, as the head of government, that he had no choice but to get involved in foreign policy. "I felt it was the duty of a middle power like Canada, which could not sway the world with the force of its armies, to at least try to sway the world with the force of its ideals. I wanted to run Canada by applying the principles of justice and equality, and I wanted our foreign policy to reflect similar values."

He made formal visits to all the major nations of the world, got Canada accepted into the Group of Seven, and made foreign aid a large part of his policies. In 1969–1970,

Canada had allocated just .3 percent of its Gross National Product (GNP) to official development assistance. By 1975, that contribution had climbed to .54 percent or $760 million. In 1978, Trudeau started opening the aid spigot more (by 1984–1985 foreign aid shot to two billion dollars with 30 percent of the aid going to the world's most destitute nations), and he called for another election in the coming March.

Margaret, who lived in a third floor suite at 24 Sussex Drive when she was in Ottawa, was by now jetting back and forth across the Atlantic regularly. When she was home, she quarreled with her estranged husband over money and gossiped with friends about her new lifestyle. She had taken bit parts in low-budget movies shot in Montréal and the south of France, and attempted a brief foray as a freelance photographer for *People Magazine.*

Trudeau had grown tired of all the bickering, at home and in Parliament. He approached Margaret about reconciliation, even vowing to leave politics and Ottawa if that would help the marriage. At first Margaret agreed, but by the end of the year she backed out from their arrangement. To Margaret, the marriage had no future. As well as giving interviews to the media exposing their relationship's difficulties, she decided to tell her own story in book form. With the help of a ghostwriter, Caroline Moorehead, Margaret transformed a series of tape-recorded interviews into a book, *Beyond Reason,* and launched it to coincide with the beginning of Trudeau's next election campaign.

It hit the press in a lurid splash of headlines just as Trudeau started electioneering about the Constitution and Canada's future. The book certainly didn't help his cause. The Trudeau government was described by its political opponents as exhausted, incompetent, and unprincipled, and the Liberals barely managed to stop the Tories from gaining a majority victory. Trudeau faced the sombre crowd of Liberals gathered in the Chateau Laurier Ballroom after the election and bravely promised his government would rise again to fight another day. The day after the election, however, his pledge was almost lost in the newspaper beside pictures of Margaret, who'd been dancing the night away in New York's Studio 54 nightclub as Trudeau had accepted his election humiliation.

Trudeau reached back to the comforts of his youth once he'd moved the boys, now aged eight, six, and four, from 24 Sussex to Stornoway, the state-provided home of the opposition leader. He undertook an arduous canoe trip in the Northwest Territories, paddling all day for an entire week with men half his age. He let his beard grow, took a trip to Tibet and China, and attempted to "dive back into the pool" by dating glamorous Canadian classical guitarist Liona Boyd. He also relaxed into a prolonged state of fatherhood that summer, taking his sons to western Canada on a tour of national parks.

As the fall approached, when he knew he'd have to return to Ottawa, Trudeau began contemplating retirement from politics to spend more time with his family, as John Turner had done. After his defeat at the polls he knew an Anglo contingent in the Liberals was fomenting a call for his departure anyway. The French component of the Party was no less dissatisfied, debating internally over the best date for a leadership review. Trudeau had become more withdrawn and was, intermittently, depressed. "I could imagine someone else being prime minister," he wrote, "but I couldn't imagine anyone else being the father of my children."

"My thinking finally crystallized at a Liberal Party convention in Toronto in November 1979. I had visited a friend in the Beaches area of Toronto, and I decided to walk all the way back to my downtown hotel. As I walked — at first along the boardwalk beside the chilly deserted beach — I reviewed all the arguments in my mind. I knew that I had to decide soon whether I was going to leave or not. I remember thinking that walking on the beach as a free man is pretty desirable."

On November 21, three days before the Liberal National Executive Committee was to call for a convention, he decided he would resign. In his opinion, Joe Clark would have a brief taste of power. He expected an inevitable election would be called within six months, when the Conservatives bungled their leadership of the country. He wanted to provide his own party with enough time to choose a new leader before it was forced to go back to the voters by the inept Tories. His prediction was correct.

Clark was slow to organize his government. The Tory

organization, new to power, was as yet undisciplined. Trudeau reasoned that if Clark made the mistake of presenting a budget that contained any major tax changes when he convened Parliament, the Conservative government stood a better than fair chance of falling to a non-confidence vote. Clark could have postponed his budget, but he wanted to show the Canadian people the Conservatives were just as equipped to run the country as the Liberals. The Tory leader allowed his finance minister, John Crosbie, to present a budget that contained a four-cent per litre hike in the gasoline tax. This was after Trudeau had been using state intervention to keep Canadian oil prices below international levels.

When Parliament was convened on December 13, many of the Conservative MPs were still busy in their ridings and not present in the House to vote for Crosbie's budget. Trudeau had been counting chairs and smiling. Clark's error in procedures, not ensuring he had the necessary bench strength for the vote, was a neophyte's mistake. Trudeau got the Liberal machine churning at top speed and in full gear. Liberal MPs from all across the country were quietly ordered to get to Ottawa and not to miss the vote under any circumstances. The Liberal call to arms was tremendous. They hired private planes and drove through the night at the command of their leader. One MP was even rushed to his seat from the hospital in an ambulance. When it came time for a vote on Crosbie's budget, the Tory government fell to the Liberal strength —133 to 139.

Clark was forced to call for an immediate election. He

counted on the country seeing Trudeau's Machiavellian manoeuvres as no better than an arrogant attempt to steal the chance to rule away from his government. He set the date for February 18, 1980.

The Liberals were suddenly vaulted into a fractious debate about whether "yesterday's man" should be asked to resume the leadership. Many looked upon Trudeau, and his marriage, as an election liability. Margaret's shenanigans were still hot news. In its September issue, *Playgirl*, a magazine known best for its centrefolds of nude men, had published an interview with her. In it, Margaret was unabashedly honest, describing her indulgences in celebrity lovemaking. Brief relationships with celebrities such as tennis star Vitas Gerulaitis and actors Jack Nicholson, Warren Beatty, and Ryan O'Neil were brought to memory for the readers. She also confessed to having an abortion as a teen. Added to that, *High Society*, a men's sex magazine, had published unusually indiscreet photos of Margaret in a New York nightclub.

Trudeau, his detractors said, was Canada's most famous cuckold. Would the electorate see a man with the personal albatross of such a lurid failed marriage as capable of running the country? Here was a woman, they were reminded, who on several occasions had become more newsworthy than the prime minister ... for not wearing a traditional floor-length gown at an official White House dinner ... for playing at being Cuban president Fidel Castro's photographer-for-a-day ... for embarrassing the nation with public outbursts that included shouting "the four-letter word" at her husband in front of diplomats in Japan.

Pierre knew what was being whispered behind his back and he bit his tongue. Finally, when asked if he would consider returning to the leadership, he gave an oblique answer. He told the Liberal caucus a story about a former prime minister in the Yunan province of China who had been asked by the emperor to return. "I've had enough of it," Pierre said. "I will come back only if the emperor asks three times on bended knee." Then he left, curbing his anger at the slights against Margaret and his marriage.

The Liberals argued amongst themselves for a while, but eventually they did ask three times. First it was the caucus who begged him to come back. Then it was the executive of the Party, and last it was Gérard Pelletier. Conversely, his friends Marc Lalonde and Jean Marchand had advised him against returning. All in all, it made Trudeau uncertain.

On a long walk around Rockcliffe Park, Trudeau considered the matter privately and decided to say no. Perhaps his subconscious was still chewing on the question overnight as he slept. Perhaps it was only his stubborn streak, but something changed his mind by the next day. Trudeau knew that Réne Lévesque, who had come to power for another term in Québec on a platform of good government rather than separatism, had cunningly waited for him to disappear from the political arena before announcing his real intention: to put separatism back to the people via a referendum vote in his province. Trudeau also knew that, once he was out of the government, he could not effectively fight against that campaign. At age 60, he wanted the opportunity history was offering him to slay the separatist dragon once and for all. On the morning of December 18, he called his closest advisors and gave them the news.

Margaret's tell-all book had detailed the tragic outcome of what can happen when two willful and self-centred people try to make a marriage work. The scenes behind the curtains of privacy Trudeau kept so carefully closed were flung open. And they shocked thc nation. Upon reading the book, many Canadians felt pity for the young flower child's baptism of fire alongside their arrogant prime minister. The marriage she described may have been sad, but her life after it's publication was just as lamentable. She had begun taking heavy doses of lithium, a mood-altering drug prescribed as therapy for her emotional problems. There were reports she had battled anorexia for a time. Money continued to be a nagging stress in her life. Her freelance photography career was a shambles and her book publisher had slipped into bankruptcy without paying the royalties she was owed. Despite Margaret's penury, Pierre was not generous with money.

During the New Year period of 1981, Trudeau took his boys to Montréal to see a spectacular art deco house built by French-Canadian architect Ernest Cormier. Trudeau had bought it, furniture and all, in anticipation of his retirement. Margaret, who was also in Montréal, was going to drive back with Trudeau and the boys to Ottawa. The night before they were to return, with the boys tucked into bed, Margaret nervously approached Trudeau with a question. As the election was coming up, it would be necessary for her to take care of the boys almost exclusively and she politely asked if he would assist by contributing to the extra cost of their keep. Trudeau smiled. "Of course," he said, tugging his wallet from his jacket. "Will $50 do?"

His heartless response was a crucible moment for Margaret. She erupted in a white-hot fury. Screaming, she physically attacked Trudeau. In the tussle that followed, he attempted to hold her down, all the while shouting orders for her to stay calm. Their angry voices awoke the children, and to both parents' shame and dismay, Sasha and Michel were witness to domestic violence. Trudeau spent a half-hour talking to a very upset four-year-old Michel before finally leaving. That night marked the irretrievable end to their marriage.

Chapter 9
Welcome to the 1980s

On the election trail, Trudeau's campaign team noticed a sudden difference in "the boss." He'd taken on a more mellow persona and appeared less prone to his fits of pique. They described him as more "whole" somehow. Was it because on a deep personal level, Trudeau realized he had finally failed at something important to him, his marriage? Perhaps it was because the emotional injury of that failure balanced his character more. He faced the Conservatives with the cold calculating skill of a seasoned warrior. He campaigned on the left, attacking the Tories for caving in to US-dominated oil companies in their policies for oil and gas. Instead of Clark's approach, Trudeau pledged Canadianization of the energy industry. He dominated the press coverage and did a tap dance of rhetoric and humour when set among hecklers. Under Trudeau's glare, Clark came across as well-meaning but ineffectual. The media labelled him "Joe Who?"

On the separatism question in Québec, Clark told the electorate he thought Canada was a "community of communities" rather than a federation. That succeeded in pushing every one of Trudeau's hot buttons. With a vengeance, Trudeau argued that Canada was greater than that. And the public recognized the force of true emotion in his words.

Though business hated Trudeau for what they perceived as a left-leaning government, and unions still hated Trudeau for the wage-and-price control program of 1975, Canada responded to the patriotic chord Trudeau plucked. They sent the Liberals back to Ottawa with a decisive majority government. Trudeau took to the stage in the Chateau Laurier after the win was declared and, smiling broadly, said, "Welcome to the 1980s!"

For his next term as prime minister he decided to focus on Québec referendum, the energy issue, the economy, and the Constitution. Privately, he also determined that he would personally follow Seneca's practical philosophy and live every day as though it was his last. "By the time I returned to office in 1980, I had learned the lessons of politics," Trudeau later wrote. "I knew you could not exhaust yourself on every issue that came along. That if you hoped to accomplish those things that were of principal importance to you, you had to compromise." Trudeau meant it literally.

Once he was back in the PMO, he asked to see NDP leader Ed Broadbent and offered to bring New Democratic Party MPs into the Cabinet in an effort to negotiate some sort of alliance with Broadbent's party. Broadbent, secure in the support his party had in the West, declined out of concern that the NDP would lose credibility with voters. After the federal election, Rene Lévesque put the matter of how the pending Québec referendum question should be structured to the politicians. The Québec National Assembly was locked in debate from March 4 to March 20 over syntax. They decided to frame the question in a long convoluted form that opponents to separation saw as an attempt to get Québec's people to agree to separatism by degree.

At first, Trudeau put his faith in the "No" campaign in the hands of Claude Ryan, leader of the Québec Liberal Party. When it appeared the "No" side was failing to gather support, he decided to step forward and speak on the issue himself, though he did so only four times. Trudeau's argument was simple. "They are asking you whether to say yes to a question that you can't honestly answer," he told French Canadians. "They are asking you whether you want an association with the other provinces, but how can your vote in Québec force the other provinces to want to associate with you if you separate?" The logic was hard to refute, especially when Trudeau made sure Quebecers heard the answer English-speaking Canada gave when asked if they would support association with an independent Québec. The answer was "No."

Lévesque responded emotionally and made a grave blunder which turned many waffling supporters towards the Trudeau camp. He said, "His name is Pierre Elliott Trudeau and this is the Elliott side taking over, and that's the English side, so we French-Canadians in Québec can't expect any sympathy from him." By saying that, Lévesque intimated someone with an English name could not be a true Quebecer. It was a strong suggestion of separatist intolerance to come if French Canadians voted yes.

Trudeau promised that a "No" vote would mean change. He pledged to bring home a new constitution with a charter of rights and an amending formula. When the referendum votes were counted, 59.6 percent were piled on the "no" side and the prime minister wasted no time. The next morning he dispatched Jean Chrétien with the command to "sell our package to the provinces." While Chrétien did his best, the effort was futile. No matter how Chrétien tried, whenever negotiations got close to the possibility of success, Québec refused to sign the Constitutional Accord or the provinces angled to erode more rights that Trudeau saw as federal. Finally, feeling that the matter would never be resolved, Trudeau decided to test his caucus with an idea. Would they support unilateral action? Would they let him take the process of patriating the Constitution out of provincial hands and allow him to go straight to Great Britain, without provincial support, providing there was an

Her Majesty Queen Elizabeth II with Prime Minister
Pierre Trudeau signing the Constitution on April 17, 1982

amending formula that gave the provinces the right to veto constitutional changes? To his satisfaction, after lengthy debate, the caucus gave its approval. In Cabinet the only key issue was whether to entrench a new Charter of Rights and Freedoms. Similar to the American Bill of Rights, the Charter of Rights and Freedoms asserted federal control in an area previously reserved under the British North America Act for the provinces. And that was civil rights.

On October 2, 1980, Trudeau faced the nation through a

television broadcast and reported successful deliberations with Great Britain's Parliament. The Constitution would finally come home.

The Constitution Act of 1982 was proclaimed on April 17. Queen Elizabeth II arrived that day and signed it into law. By patriating the Constitution and its entrenched Charter of Rights and Freedoms, Trudeau severed Canada's last colonial links with Britain.

Chapter 10
The Statesman Departs

Trudeau believed he'd accomplished almost everything he'd set out to achieve with the Constitution and the Charter of Rights and Freedoms, but he still felt one matter, more global, still demanded his attention. Nuclear proliferation.

For most of his political life, Trudeau had been a vocal critic of the military Cold War chess match. The United States and Soviet policies of nuclear deterrent had taken the world to the verge of annihilation several times since the Cuban Missile Crisis. In 1978, he presented a detailed speech to the United Nations on a strategy of "nuclear suffocation." He called for an immediate halt to all laboratory development of weapon systems and for international efforts to reduce stockpiles of nuclear weapons. He told diplomats from around the world that Canada was not only the first country that chose not to build nuclear weapons, it was also the first nuclear-armed country that had chosen to get rid of them.

His strategy for peace was not well received by his North Atlantic Treaty Organization (NATO) partners. NATO was committed to matching the Warsaw Pact countries gun for gun. The Soviets had introduced a powerful new SS–20 missile and NATO wanted to counter that threat with new American-designed cruise missiles. Those missiles needed practical testing over geography similar to what would be encountered on a low altitude attack. To his chagrin, Trudeau accepted that, as part of the NATO organization, Canada had to allow cruise missile testing over its soil. That decision had made him look insincere about his anti-proliferation scheme, but it also focussed his attention even more on the threats of nuclear war.

In the summer of 1983, Trudeau decided it was time to move forward aggressively with an international peace initiative that could perhaps end the Cold War. He put together a task force which distilled his 26 ideas into five ways Canada might help to get East and West talking peace: renewed dialogue at a proposed Stockholm conference on disarmament; a stronger non-proliferation treaty; reduction of conventional armed forces in Europe; a five-power disarmament conference; and, a ban on high-altitude testing of anti-satellite missiles.

On a capital-hopping trip around the world, Trudeau tried to gain support for his initiatives from all nuclear-armed countries. Not surprisingly, his unsolicited suggestions were not met with enthusiasm. India rejected non-proliferation. Britain rejected a disarmament conference. Trudeau had, however, managed to meet all the leaders and from his efforts, a dialogue between them soon emerged. What resulted was a concerted global effort to limit nuclear arms. On February 9, 1984, Trudeau reported his efforts to the House of Commons. "Let it be said of Canada and of Canadians that we saw the crisis; that we did act; that we took risks; that we were loyal to our friends and open with our adversaries; that we have lived up to our ideal; and that we have done what we could to lift the shadow of war."

The long hours of solitude on airplanes during his global mission had given him plenty of time to consider his future as well. Not long after his speech, he decided to take a walk by himself, this time in a raging Ottawa blizzard, to make a decision about retirement once again. He and Margaret had gotten divorced that year. Soon after, Margaret married Ottawa real-estate developer Fred Kemper and started a new life that later would include two more children.

"My three boys were entering their teens and I felt the need to spend more time with them," Trudeau recalled. "For all their lives until then, from the moment each of them was born, they had been the prime minister's children, set apart from others by that fact, accompanied by bodyguards and so on. I wanted them to spend at least their teenage years as ordinary youngsters in Montréal, entirely away from public life. I also didn't know whether I had the energy left to fight another grueling election campaign."

The next day he stepped down for the last time. Upon retirement, Pierre moved his boys to the art deco house he'd bought on Pine Avenue in Montréal in 1979. And he moved out of the public eye. He took time to scuba dive and canoe. He treated his boys to trips in France, Ireland and Scotland, China, and Southeast Asia. Still only 65 and eager to keep working, he accepted a position as senior counsel at Heenan Blaikie law firm in Montréal. Until October 1995, Trudeau's presence in the public was limited to interviews he gave reporters, but at 76 years old, he emerged from his privacy. Once again he argued against another separatist referendum in his province and once again — though only by a .6 percent majority — saw it fail.

The years after 1995 still held reminders of his vitality and moments of deep sorrow through which Canadians shared their condolences. It was revealed that on May 5, 1991, Trudeau had fathered a daughter, Sarah, with prominent Liberal Party constitutional lawyer, Deborah Coyne. Coyne was 36. He was 71. It had been a secret he kept more closely than many others, and friends that knew him kept it well. They had learned that if Pierre thought you had divulged private information, he would swiftly distance you. During his political career, he had not even allowed himself the pleasure of socializing with Cabinet colleagues in his home unless a state occasion demanded it.

The lawyers he worked with at Heenan Blaikie were particularly aware of his devotion to all of the children, including Sarah. It took only a few moments for a client visiting his Montréal law office to realize the children were at the centre of his life and never far from his thoughts. But colleagues rarely spoke of the children outside their private circle. Trudeau's children were nobody's business but his.

Then, on November 13, 1998, Pierre and Margaret's youngest son, 23-year-old Michel, died tragically in an avalanche that swept him to the bottom of Kokanee Lake in British Columbia. The entire country reached out with their hearts to the grieving parents. Michel had reportedly been crossing a slope above Kokanee Lake in Kokanee Glacier Park when the avalanche occurred. He was an adventure lover, like his father. Michel had been working beneath the radar of the press as a ski-lift attendant in Rossland before his sudden tragic death. Trudeau's friends said he never recovered from the loss.

Neither did Margaret. "I miss him every day, but I understand that death is part of life," she told a newspaper. "I've survived the worst of it. Such horror no one can survive without faith." Margaret separated from her second husband soon after Michel's death. Reportedly, it was a key factor in the separation. Margaret later became active with WaterCan, an Ottawa-based organization dedicated to providing clean drinking water in developing countries, and she began working on avalanche awareness through the Canadian Avalanche Association.

In a way, perhaps, Michel's death served as a strengthening bond for his survivors. Margaret and Pierre met often, after Michel was gone, to discuss their children. And they eventually built a close friendship that surpassed the pain of their divorce.

On September 7, 2000, word reached Canada that the Canadian icon — as much a symbol of Canada as the maple leaf — was dying. Within hours, the eyes of the nation were fixed on the door to his art deco mansion on the southwest slope of Mount Royal. The man that Canadian newspaper editors and broadcasters named "Canada's newsmaker of the century" was drifting away.

Roses, the symbol of his insouciance for so many years, were piled at his doorstep. And Canadians across the country shared their memories. Some didn't hide their continued hatred for him. They vilified him for a crippling national debt they said Canada could never repay. Albertans reminded their neighbours of his crippling NEP debacle and that his view was very much an Ottawa–Montréal–Toronto sense of the country. Québecers, depending on their separatist position, said René Lévesque most epitomized who they were. Trudeau, however, was most like what they wanted to be. Some Canadians were kinder and acknowledged that, despite their disagreement with his vision, they respected his intellect. He was a poet, they said. He spoke to the hearts of a nation. The opinions were as varied as Canada. But for the most part, Canadians prepared themselves to grieve the loss of their most outstanding native son, a man everyone could agree had truly changed their country.

The day after his death, in the late afternoon, a note was given to the press. "Justin and Sacha Trudeau deeply regret to inform you that their father, the Right Honourable Pierre Elliott Trudeau, passed away shortly after 3:00 p.m. today, September 28, 2000. In addition to Parkinson's disease, Mr. Trudeau suffered from prostate cancer."

More than 13,000 people filed past Trudeau's casket as he lay in state at Montreal City Hall. The line-up was three hours long. In Ottawa, more than 60,000 paid their respects. His funeral was reported by the Canadian media with sympathy. Opportunities for long, lurid exposés of the family's private lives were avoided by the television networks. Newspapers and television reporters offered time and space for Canadians to remember *their* prime minister with personal stories instead. The symbolic gesture epitomized that elusive Canadian quality that seems to escape definition by anyone who doesn't live here. In other countries, the funeral would have turned into a media frenzy, but in Canada it humbly marked an ending moment in our history. Cameras barely flitted over the faces of Justin, Sacha, and Sarah as Roman Catholic Archbishop of Montréal, Jean-Claude Cardinal Turcotte, extended his condolences at Notre-Dame Basilica.

The grand basilica in the heart of Old Montréal was filled with politicians, old and new, close friends, and grieving family. Though the sombre proceedings were distant and reserved for only a few, all of Canada still felt a part of that ceremony. Canadians crowded around television sets wherever they were. In sports bars and shopping malls. In school auditoriums and living rooms. They observed in silence. While Cuban President Fidel Castro hugged the boys, and former U.S. president Jimmy Carter embraced nine-year-old Sarah, Canadians wept. Across the nation, tributes were made. Church bells tolled. Office work stopped as a moment of silence was taken by workers of every stripe for their *gunslinger* prime minister. There was a visceral outpouring of grief. The Centennial Flame on Parliament Hill, which had become a shrine to Trudeau, was turned off for days because so many flowers had been heaped upon it. And when Justin Trudeau quietly gave his father's eulogy, Canada listened in a hush 5000 kilometres wide.

The young man described his dad in a manner both genuine and personal. He talked of how, as a six-year-old, he'd accompanied his father to Alert. The only child in Canada's northernmost scientific outpost, he'd felt despondent because the time he'd hoped to spend with his father was elusive. He spoke of the formless Arctic waste. His boredom. He remembered how one day he'd been taken to a small red shack and boosted up to a window, and there given a brief glimpse of a man in a red suit who was busy building toys, his grinning father. Justin let Canada share a smile over a private moment that eloquently marked the playful side of the man they were all grieving. And he gave them a glimpse of his father's character as well.

Justin spoke of a day his father taught him the meaning of respect. The two were sharing a meal in the parliamentary restaurant when Justin, eight years old, recognized one of Trudeau's political rivals seated nearby. "Thinking of pleasing my father, I told a joke about him – a generic, silly little grade school thing. My father looked at me sternly with that look I would learn to know so well, and said, 'Justin, never attack the individual. One can be in total disagreement with someone without denigrating him as a consequence.'

"Saying that, he stood up and took me by the hand and brought me over to introduce me to this man. He was a nice man who was eating with his daughter, a nice-looking blond girl a little younger than I was. My father's adversary spoke to me in a friendly manner and it was then that I understood that having different opinions from those of another person in no way precluded holding this person in the highest respect. Because mere tolerance is not enough: we must have true and deep respect for every human being, regardless of his beliefs, his origins, and his values. That is what my father demanded of his sons and that is what he demanded of our country."

Canadians lined the route on Trudeau's final journey. As train Number 638 passed through stations, they reached out to touch the black-curtained car bearing his flag-draped coffin. They sang "O Canada" in both English and French.

Pierre Elliott Trudeau was buried next to his mother in a private ceremony attended only by family.

Epilogue

The life of this great Canadian statesman is a chronicle of both stellar achievements and significant failures. Trudeau modernized Canada's divorce law, introduced official bilingualism, created a ministry to protect our environment, and introduced tax policies that forced Canadians to consider their future retirement. He patriated our Constitution, cutting Canada's colonial ties to Great Britain, and he entrenched a Charter of Rights and Freedoms by which all Canadians now live.

He enforced the state's power on a groaning nation with wage and price controls. He discounted the importance of the long-term cost implications created by a ballooning federal deficit. He created pork-barrel job creation schemes, alienated westerners with a restrictive National Energy Program, and often cared too little about the problems of prairie farmers or East Coast fishermen.

He wasn't above showing his anger with a curse, or beneath showing compassion with a prayer. But in the balance, taking it all into consideration — the good, the bad, the mystery, the arrogance — he was a man of true greatness.

With his outstanding capacity to envision a better

world, with the power of his intellect and his sheer passion and will, Pierre Elliott Trudeau gave us all the briefest glimpse of what it means to be a Canadian.

Bibliography

Axworthy, Thomas S. *Towards a Just Society: The Trudeau Years.* Edited by Pierre Elliot Trudeau. Markham, Ontario: Penguin Books Canada Ltd. 1990.

Finkel, Alvin. *Our Lives: Canada After 1945.* Toronto, Ontario: James Lorimer & Company Ltd., 1997.

Graham, Ron, ed., *Trudeau: The Essential Trudeau.* Toronto, Ontario: McClelland and Stewart Inc. 1998.

Gwyn, Richard. *The Northern Magus.* Toronto, Ontario: McClelland and Stewart Inc., 1980.

McRoberts, Kenneth. *Misconceiving Canada: the Struggle for National Unity.* Don Mills, Ontario: Oxford University Press, 1997.

Palmer, Howard with Tamara Palmer. *Alberta: A New History.* Edmonton, Alberta: Hurtig Publishers, 1990.

Pearson, Lester B. *Mike: The Memoirs Of The Right Honourable Lester B. Pearson.* Volume 1. Toronto, Ontario: University of Toronto Press, 1972.

Powe, B.W. *The Solitary Outlaw.* Toronto, Ontario: Lester and Orpen Dennys, 1987.

Radwanski, George. *Trudeau.* Toronto, Ontario: Macmillan of Canada, 1977.

Trofimenkoff, Susan Mann. *The Dream of Nation: A Social and Intellectual History of Québec.* Toronto, Ontario: Gage, 1983.

Trudeau, Margaret. *Beyond Reason.* New York, N.Y.: Paddington Press, 1979.

Trudeau, Pierre Elliott. *Memoirs.* Toronto, Ontario: McClelland and Stewart Inc., 1993.

Trudeau, Pierre Elliott. *The Essential Trudeau.* Edited by Ron Graham. Toronto, Ontario: McClelland and Stewart Inc., 1998.

Wade, Mason. *The French Canadians, Volume Two: 1911–1967,* revised edition. Toronto, Ontario: Macmillan of Canada, 1968.

Acknowledgments

I would like to acknowledge the kind assistance of all the librarians I pestered during the research for this book. Trying to distill the life of a Canadian icon in so few words was a taxing effort. I would have found it impossible without their help.

Photo Credits

Cover: D. Cameron / National Archives of Canada (PA-111213); D. Cameron / National Archives of Canada: page 56 (PA-117107); National Archives of Canada: page 67 (PA-180808), page 87 (PA-143959), 117 (PA-141503).

About the Author

Stan Sauerwein lives and writes in Westbank, British Columbia. A freelance writer for two decades, his articles have appeared in a variety of Canadian and US magazines and newspapers. Specializing in business subjects, he has written for both corporations and governments. He is also the author of *Rattenbury: The Life and Tragic End of BC's Greatest Architect*; *Ma Murray: The Story of Canada's Crusty Queen of Publishing*; *Klondike Joe Boyle: Heroic Adventures from Gold Fields to Battlefields*; *Moe Norman: The Canadian Golfing Legend with the Perfect Swing*; and *Fintry: Lives, Loves and Dreams.*

AMAZING STORIES
by the same author

Rattenbury
ISBN 1-55153-981-0

AMAZING STORIES

by the same author

Klondike Joe Boyle

ISBN 1-55153-969-1

AMAZING STORIES

by the same author

Ma Murray

ISBN 1-55153-979-9

AMAZING STORIES

by the same author

Moe Norman
ISBN 1-55153-953-5

AMAZING STORIES

NOW AVAILABLE!

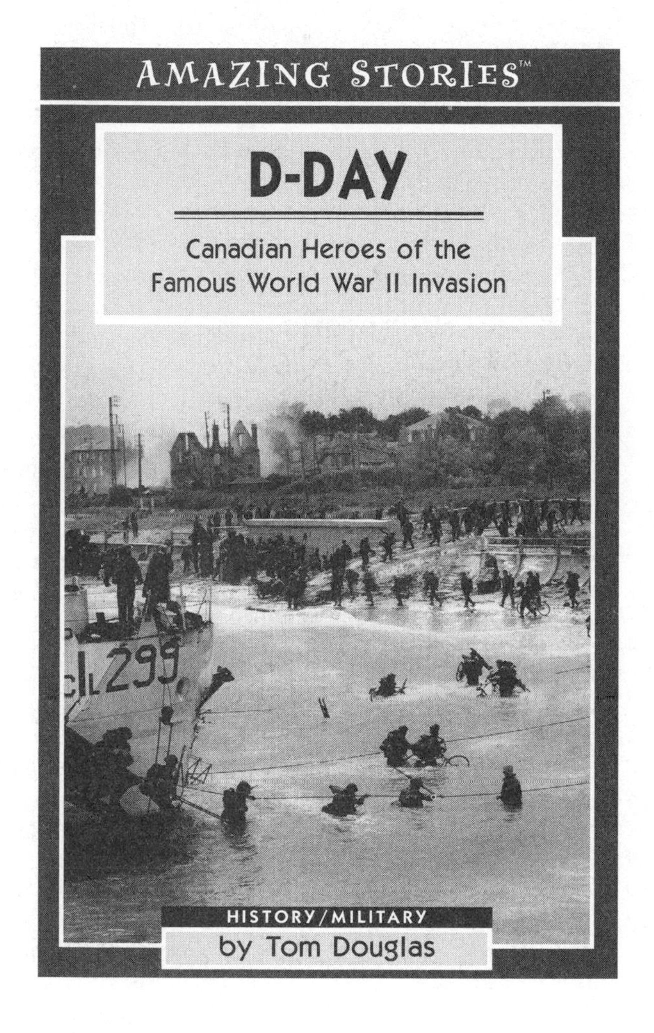

D-Day

ISBN 1-55153-795-8

OTHER AMAZING STORIES

ISBN	Title
1-55153-959-4	A War Bride's Story
1-55153-794-X	Calgary Flames
1-55153-947-0	Canada's Rumrunners
1-55153-966-7	Canadian Spies
1-55153-795-8	D-Day
1-55153-972-1	David Thompson
1-55153-982-9	Dinosaur Hunters
1-55153-970-5	Early Voyageurs
1-55153-798-2	Edmonton Oilers
1-55153-968-3	Edwin Alonzo Boyd
1-55153-996-9	Emily Carr
1-55153-961-6	Étienne Brûlé
1-55153-791-5	Extraordinary Accounts of Native Life on the West Coast
1-55153-992-6	Ghost Town Stories II
1-55153-984-5	Ghost Town Stories III
1-55153-993-4	Ghost Town Stories
1-55153-973-X	Great Canadian Love Stories
1-55153-777-X	Great Cat Stories
1-55153-946-2	Great Dog Stories
1-55153-773-7	Great Military Leaders
1-55153-785-0	Grey Owl
1-55153-958-6	Hudson's Bay Company Adventures
1-55153-969-1	Klondike Joe Boyle
1-55153-980-2	Legendary Show Jumpers
1-55153-775-3	Lucy Maud Montgomery
1-55153-967-5	Marie Anne Lagimodière
1-55153-964-0	Marilyn Bell
1-55153-999-3	Mary Schäffer
1-55153-953-5	Moe Norman
1-55153-965-9	Native Chiefs and Famous Métis
1-55153-962-4	Niagara Daredevils
1-55153-793-1	Norman Bethune
1-55153-951-9	Ontario Murders
1-55153-790-7	Ottawa Senators
1-55153-960-8	Ottawa Titans
1-55153-945-4	Pierre Elliot Trudeau
1-55153-981-0	Rattenbury
1-55153-991-8	Rebel Women
1-55153-995-0	Rescue Dogs
1-55153-985-3	Riding on the Wild Side
1-55153-974-8	Risk Takers and Innovat
1-55153-956-X	Robert Service
1-55153-799-0	Roberta Bondar
1-55153-997-7	Sam Steele
1-55153-954-3	Snowmobile Adventure
1-55153-971-3	Stolen Horses
1-55153-952-7	Strange Events
1-55153-783-4	Strange Events and Mor
1-55153-986-1	Tales from the West Coa
1-55153-978-0	The Avro Arrow Story
1-55153-943-8	The Black Donnellys
1-55153-942-X	The Halifax Explosion
1-55153-994-2	The Heart of a Horse
1-55153-944-6	The Life of a Loyalist
1-55153-787-7	The Mad Trapper
1-55153-789-3	The Mounties
1-55153-948-9	The War of 1812 Again the States
1-55153-788-5	Toronto Maple Leafs
1-55153-976-4	Trailblazing Sports Heroes
1-55153-977-2	Unsung Heroes of the Royal Canadian Air For
1-55153-792-3	Vancouver Canucks
1-55153-989-6	Vancouver's Old-Time Scoundrels
1-55153-990-X	West Coast Adventures
1-55153-987-X	Wilderness Tales
1-55153-873-3	Women Explorers

These titles are available wherever you buy books. If you have trouble finding the book you want, call the Altitude order desk at **1-800-957-6888**, e-mail your request to: **orderdesk@altitudepublishing.com** or visit our Web site at **www.amazingstories.ca**

New **AMAZING STORIES** titles are published every month.